THE INTERNET

FOR

MACS™

FOR

DUMMIES®

Quick Reference
2nd Edition

THE INTERNET
FOR
MACS™
FOR
DUMMIES®

Quick Reference
2nd Edition

by Dan Parks Sydow

IDG
BOOKS
WORLDWIDE

IDG Books Worldwide, Inc.
An International Data Group Company

Foster City, CA ✦ Chicago, IL ✦ Indianapolis, IN ✦ Braintree, MA ✦ Southlake, TX

The Internet For Macs™ For Dummies® Quick Reference, 2nd Edition

Published by
IDG Books Worldwide, Inc.
An International Data Group Company
919 E. Hillsdale Blvd.
Suite 400
Foster City, CA 94404

Library of Congress Catalog Card No.: 95-78770

ISBN: 1-56884-983-4

Printed in the United States of America

10 9 8 7 6 5 4 3 2 1

2A/SY/QS/ZW/IN

Distributed in the United States by IDG Books Worldwide, Inc.

Distributed by Macmillan Canada for Canada; by Computer and Technical Books for the Caribbean Basin; by Contemporanea de Ediciones for Venezuela; by Distribuidora Cuspide for Argentina; by CITEC for Brazil; by Ediciones ZETA S.C.R. Ltda. for Peru; by Editorial Limusa SA for Mexico; by Transworld Publishers Limited in the United Kingdom and Europe; by Al-Maiman Publishers & Distributors for Saudi Arabia; by Simron Pty. Ltd. for South Africa; by IDG Communications (HK) Ltd. for Hong Kong; by Toppan Company Ltd. for Japan; by Addison Wesley Publishing Company for Korea; by Longman Singapore Publishers Ltd. for Singapore, Malaysia, Thailand, and Indonesia; by Unalis Corporation for Taiwan; by WS Computer Publishing Company, Inc. for the Philippines; by WoodsLane Pty. Ltd. for Australia; by WoodsLane Enterprises Ltd. for New Zealand.

For general information on IDG Books Worldwide's books in the U.S., please call our Consumer Customer Service department at 800-762-2974. For reseller information, including discounts and premium sales, please call our Reseller Customer Service department at 800-434-3422.

For information on where to purchase IDG Books Worldwide's books outside the U.S., contact IDG Books Worldwide at 415-655-3021 or fax 415-655-3295.

For information on translations, contact Marc Jeffrey Mikulich, Director, Foreign & Subsidiary Rights, at IDG Books Worldwide, 415-655-3018 or fax 415-655-3295.

For sales inquiries and special prices for bulk quantities, write to the address above or call IDG Books Worldwide at 415-655-3200.

For information on using IDG Books Worldwide's books in the classroom, or ordering examination copies, contact the Education Office at 800-434-2086 or fax 817-251-8174.

For authorization to photocopy items for corporate, personal, or educational use, please contact Copyright Clearance Center, 222 Rosewood Drive, Danvers, MA 01923, or fax 508-750-4470.

is a trademark under exclusive license
to IDG Books Worldwide, Inc.,
from International Data Group, Inc.

About the Author

Dan Parks Sydow

Dan Parks Sydow is a graduate of the Milwaukee School of Engineering with a degree in Computer Engineering. He has worked on software in several diverse areas, including the display of images of the heart for medical purposes. Since Dan can't stand the sight of blood — even electronic blood — he quit his nine-to-five job as a software engineer to become a freelance writer and consultant.

Dan got hooked on Macintosh programming ten years ago when the Macintosh was first introduced. Since then, he has spared no effort in avoiding all other types of computers. He enjoys shedding light on topics that people have been led to believe were beyond their reach and has written several computer programming books — all dealing with the Macintosh.

WINNER
Eighth Annual
Computer Press
Awards ⪢ 1992

WINNER
Ninth Annual
Computer Press
Awards ⪢ 1993

Welcome to the world of IDG Books Worldwide.

IDG Books Worldwide, Inc., is a subsidiary of International Data Group, the world's largest publisher of computer-related information and the leading global provider of information services on information technology. IDG was founded more than 25 years ago and now employs more than 7,700 people worldwide. IDG publishes more than 250 computer publications in 67 countries (see listing below). More than 70 million people read one or more IDG publications each month.

Launched in 1990, IDG Books Worldwide is today the #1 publisher of best-selling computer books in the United States. We are proud to have received 8 awards from the Computer Press Association in recognition of editorial excellence and three from Computer Currents' First Annual Readers' Choice Awards, and our best-selling ...For Dummies® series has more than 19 million copies in print with translations in 28 languages. IDG Books Worldwide, through a joint venture with IDG's Hi-Tech Beijing, became the first U.S. publisher to publish a computer book in the People's Republic of China. In record time, IDG Books Worldwide has become the first choice for millions of readers around the world who want to learn how to better manage their businesses.

Our mission is simple: Every one of our books is designed to bring extra value and skill-building instructions to the reader. Our books are written by experts who understand and care about our readers. The knowledge base of our editorial staff comes from years of experience in publishing, education, and journalism — experience which we use to produce books for the '90s. In short, we care about books, so we attract the best people. We devote special attention to details such as audience, interior design, use of icons, and illustrations. And because we use an efficient process of authoring, editing, and desktop publishing our books electronically, we can spend more time ensuring superior content and spend less time on the technicalities of making books.

You can count on our commitment to deliver high-quality books at competitive prices on topics you want to read about. At IDG Books Worldwide, we continue in the IDG tradition of delivering quality for more than 25 years. You'll find no better book on a subject than one from IDG Books Worldwide.

John J. Kilcullen

John Kilcullen
President and CEO
IDG Books Worldwide, Inc.

IDG Books Worldwide, Inc., is a subsidiary of International Data Group, the world's largest publisher of computer-related information and the leading global provider of information services on information technology. International Data Group publishes over 250 computer publications in 67 countries. Seventy million people read one or more International Data Group publications each month. International Data Group's publications include: **ARGENTINA:** Computerworld Argentina, GamePro, Infoworld, PC World Argentina; **AUSTRALIA:** Australian Macworld, Client/Server Journal, Computer Living, Computerworld, Digital News, Network World, PC World, Publishing Essentials, Reseller; **AUSTRIA:** Computerwelt, PC TEST; **BELARUS:** PC World Belarus; **BELGIUM:** Data News; **BRAZIL:** Annuário de Informática, Computerworld Brazil, Connections, Super Game Power, Macworld, PC World Brazil, Publish Brazil, SUPERGAME; **BULGARIA:** Computerworld Bulgaria, Networkworld/Bulgaria, PC & MacWorld Bulgaria; **CANADA:** CIO Canada, ComputerWorld Canada, InfoCanada, Network World Canada, Reseller World; **CHILE:** Computerworld Chile, GamePro, PC World Chile; **COLUMBIA:** Computerworld Colombia, GamePro, PC World Colombia; **COSTA RICA:** PC World Costa Rica/Nicaragua; **THE CZECH AND SLOVAK REPUBLICS:** Computerworld Czechoslovakia, Elektronika Czechoslovakia, PC World Czechoslovakia; **DENMARK:** Communications World, Computerworld Danmark, Macworld Danmark, PC World Danmark, PC World Danmark Supplements, TECH World; **DOMINICAN REPUBLIC:** PC World Republica Dominicana; **ECUADOR:** PC World Ecuador, GamePro; **EGYPT:** Computerworld Middle East, PC World Middle East; **EL SALVADOR:** PC World Centro America; **FINLAND:** MikroPC, Tietoverkko, Tietoviikko; **FRANCE:** Distributique, Golden, Info PC, Le Guide du Monde Informatique, Le Monde Informatique, Reseaux & Telecoms; **GERMANY:** Computer Business, Computerwoche, Computerwoche Extra, Computerwoche Focus, Electronic Entertainment, GamePro, I/M Information Management, Macwelt, PC Welt; **GREECE:** GamePro, Macworld & Publish; **GUATEMALA:** PC World Centro America; **HONDURAS:** PC World Centro America; **HONG KONG:** Computerworld Hong Kong, PCWorld Hong Kong, Publish in Asia; **HUNGARY:** ABCD CD-ROM, Computerworld Szamitastechnika, PC & Mac World Hungary, PC-X Magazine; **INDIA:** Computerworld India, PC World India, Publish in Asia; **INDONESIA:** InfoKomputer PC World, Komputek Computerworld, Publish in Asia; **IRELAND:** ComputerScope, PC Live!; **ISRAEL:** PC World 32 BIT, People & Computers; **ITALY:** Computerworld Italia, Computerworld Italia Special Editions, Lotus Italia, Macworld Italia, Networking Italia, PC Shopping, PC World Italia, PC World/Walt Disney; **JAPAN:** Macworld Japan, Nikkei Personal Computing, SunWorld Japan, Windows World Japan; **KENYA:** East African Computer News; **KOREA:** Hi-Tech Information/Computerworld, Macworld Korea, PC World Korea; **MACEDONIA:** PC World Macedonia; **MALAYSIA:** Computerworld Malaysia, PC World Malaysia, Publish in Asia; **MEXICO:** Computerworld Mexico, GamePro, Macworld, PC World Mexico; **MYANMAR:** PC World Myanmar; **NETHERLANDS:** Computable, Computer! Totaal, LAN Magazine, Macworld, Net Magazine; **NEW ZEALAND:** Computer Buyer, Computerworld New Zealand, MTB, Network World, PC World New Zealand; **NICARAGUA:** PC World Costa Rica/Nicaragua; **NIGERIA:** PC World Africa; **NORWAY:** Computerworld Norge, Computerworld Privat, CW Rapport Klient/Tjener, CW Rapport Nettver & Telecom, CW Rapport Offentlig Sektor, IDG's KURSGUIDE, Macworld Norge, Multimedia World, PC World Ekspress, PC World Nettverk, PC World Norge, PC World's Produktguide, Windows Special; **PAKISTAN:** Computerworld Pakistan, PC World Pakistan; **PANAMA:** GamePro, PC World Panama; **PARAGUAY:** PC World Paraguay; **P. R. OF CHINA:** China Computerworld, China Infoworld, Computer de Communications, Electronic Product World, Electronics Today, Game Camp, PC World China, Popular Computer Week, Software World, Telecom Product World; **PERU:** Computerworld Peru, GamePro, PC World Profesional Peru, PC World Peru; **POLAND:** Computerworld Poland, Computerworld Special Report, Macworld, Networld, PC World Komputer; **PHILIPPINES:** Computerworld Philippines, PC Digest, Publish in Asia; **PORTUGAL:** Cerebro/PC World, Correio Informático/Computerworld, Mac*In/PC*In Portugal; **PUERTO RICO:** PC World Puerto Rico; **ROMANIA:** Computerworld Romania, PC World Romania, Telecom Romania; **RUSSIA:** Computerworld Rossiya, Network World Russia, PC World Russia; **SINGAPORE:** Computerworld Singapore, PC World Singapore, Publish in Asia; **SLOVENIA:** MONITOR; **SOUTH AFRICA:** Computing S.A., Network World S.A., Software World; **SPAIN:** Computerworld España, COMUNICACIONES WORLD, Dealer World, Macworld España, PC World España; **SWEDEN:** CAP&Design, Computer Sweden, Corporate Computing, MacWorld, Maxi Data, MikroDatorn, Nätverk & Kommunikation, PC/Aktiv, PC World, Windows World; **SWITZERLAND:** Computerworld Schweiz, Macworld Schweiz, PCtip; **TAIWAN:** Computerworld Taiwan, Macworld Taiwan, PC World Taiwan, Publish Taiwan, Windows World; **THAILAND:** Thai Computerworld, Publish in Asia; **TURKEY:** Computerworld Monitör, MACWORLD Turkiye, PC WORLD Turkiye; **UKRAINE:** Computerworld Kiev, Computers & Software Magazine, PC World Ukraine; **UNITED KINGDOM:** Acorn User, Amiga Action, Amiga Computing, Amiga, Appletalk, CD Powerplay, CD-ROM Now, Computing, Connection, GamePro, Lotus Magazine, Macaction, Macworld, Open Computing, Parents and Computers, PC Home, PC Works, The WEB; **UNITED STATES:** Cable in the Classroom, CD Review, CIO Magazine, Computerworld, Computerworld Client/Server Journal, Digital Video Magazine, DOS World, Electronic, InfoWorld, I-Way, Macworld, Maximize, MULTIMEDIA WORLD, Network World, PC World, PUBLISH, SWATPro Magazine, Video Event, WebMaster; **URUGUAY:** PC World Uruguay; **VENEZUELA:** Computerworld Venezuela, GamePro, PC World Venezuela; and **VIETNAM:** PC World Vietnam   10/17/95

Acknowledgments

I would like to thank Tim Gallan for his work as project editor of this book. I would also like to thank the IDG editorial and production staff for their efforts. A special thanks to Suzanne Packer for her detailed copyediting and numerous suggestions.

(The Publisher would like to give special thanks to Patrick S. McGovern, without whom this book wold not have been possible.)

Credits

**Senior Vice President
and Publisher**
Milissa L. Koloski

Associate Publisher
Diane Graves Steele

Brand Manager
Judith A. Taylor

Editorial Managers
Kristin A. Cocks
Mary Corder

Product Development Manager
Mary Bednarek

Editorial Executive Assistant
Richard Graves

Acquisitions Editor
Tammy Goldfeld

Assistant Acquisitions Editor
Gareth Hancock

Production Director
Beth Jenkins

Production Assistant
Jacalyn L. Pennywell

**Supervisor of
Project Coordination**
Cindy L. Phipps

Supervisor of Page Layout
Kathie S. Schnorr

Supervisor of Graphics and Design
Shelley Lea

Production Systems Specialist
Steve Peake

Reprint/Blueline Coordination
Tony Augsburger
Patricia R. Reynolds
Theresa Sánchez-Baker

Media/Archive Coordination
Leslie Popplewell
Melissa Stauffer
Michael Wilkey

Editors
Tim Gallan
Suzanne Packer

Editorial Assistants
Constance Carlisle
Chris Collins
Kevin Spencer

Technical Reviewer
Brian Combs

Associate Project Coordinator
Debbie Sharpe

Graphic Coordination
Gina Scott
Angela F. Hunckler

Production Page Layout
Cameron Booker
Elizabeth Cárdenas-Nelson
Kerri Cornell
Drew R. Moore
Kate Snell

Proofreaders
Betty Kish
Christine Meloy Beck
Gwenette Gaddis
Dwight Ramsey
Carl Saff
Robert Springer

Indexer

Table of Contents

How to Use This Book

Want a telephone-book-sized reference of every conceivable task and resource pertaining to the Internet? If so, don't look here — this reference book is short, crisp, and concise. Here, you find the information that you need to get up and running on the Internet, along with the howtos for performing basic Internet tasks that allow you to get work done and, perhaps, have a little fun. And while the Internet is an expanding, evolving entity, the subjects covered in this reference are basic enough that their descriptions will be accurate and useful for a period of time longer than it takes to e-mail suggestions for the next edition of this book!

While I won't claim that I can please *everyone,* I've tried to come pretty darn close in this book! No matter what Mac software you use (or will use) to access the Internet, the odds are that you'll find step-by-step task-solving instructions written just for you. That's possible because I provide the steps necessary to perform any one task for readers who use America Online, CompuServe, Prodigy, or eWorld.

Additionally, readers who choose to work on the Internet without going through an online service are accommodated. If you own Netscape, Eudora, NewsWatcher, Fetch, or TurboGopher software, there's plenty in this book for you, too. Perhaps most importantly, this book is written *by* a Mac user *for* Mac users.

Finally, this book's table of contents, glossary, and extensive index will also be of help regardless of the topic that you're searching for.

Finding Things in This Book

This book is divided into sections, or parts, to keep things well organized — and to help you quickly find the information that you need.

Part I, "Getting to Know the Internet," tells you what the Internet is, what the World Wide Web is, and why you *need* to become familiar with them.

Part II, "Getting Started," describes the hardware and software that you need to get connected to both the Internet and the Web.

Part III, "Electronic Mail," tells you all about sending and receiving worldwide e-mail.

Part IV, "Mailing Lists," shows you how to subscribe to a mailing list. A *mailing list* is made up of a group of people — all interested in the same topic, such as computer programming, traveling, or tropical fish — who correspond with one another.

Part V, "Newsgroups," describes Usenet newsgroups. Like a mailing list, a newsgroup is devoted to a single topic. As a mailing list participant, you receive e-mail in your own electronic mailbox. But as a newsgroup participant, you simply read messages that are posted for anyone to read.

Part VI, "File Downloading (FTP)," explains how you can get files from the Internet to your own computer. All the basics of file transfer protocol, or FTP, are covered so that you'll be able to quickly obtain text documents, utilities, and freeware and shareware programs.

Part VII, "Searching for Files," tells you how to find the information that you need from the vast expanse of the Internet. Part VI shows you how to download files — this part shows you how to find them first!

Part VIII, "The World Wide Web," introduces you to the Web — the graphical part of the Internet. Here, you see how to navigate the Web using a special type of Internet address called a *URL,* or uniform resource locator.

Part IX, "Doing Business on the Internet," describes how your business — whether big or small — can get its own place on the Internet. In particular, you get some exposure to the details of putting up your own page, or site, on the World Wide Web.

Several appendixes are included and list tons of exciting information.

You also find a glossary after the appendixes. Keep the glossary in mind as you jump about through this reference book. While terminology is explained as it is introduced, you may occasionally encounter a mystifying techie term and not recall what it means or where you first came across it.

Conventions Used in This Book

When you are expected to type something, that "something" appears in boldface. For example, if you are requested to type the word "gopher," you'll see the following:

Type **gopher**.

After typing in a command such as the one above, I'll tell you whether you should finish off by pressing the Return or Enter key, or by clicking on some appropriate button.

To set off e-mail addresses, URLS, and the like, I use a monospaced font as in the following example:

Send e-mail to `dsydow@interramp.com`.

The Cast of Icons

As you page through this reference book, you'll find icons liberally scattered about the margins. These icons help you focus on the tasks being described.

This tip will save you time. It may also help you look like an Internet pro in the eyes of other *Netters* — those countless other people surfing the Internet.

Danger! While the task that is being discussed won't send your Mac up in smoke, it may cause some sort of trouble or delay.

The task being discussed does indeed work, but perhaps not as expected. For reasons too obscure to understand, the way the discussed task is accomplished is still the way things are done on the Internet.

Follow the directions given in this shortcut to see the quickest way to complete a task.

This icon refers you to related material found in other *...For Dummies* books.

Part 1

Getting to Know the Internet

Does it seem like just yesterday that the Internet didn't exist, while today it is talked about as if it is *all* that exists? That's a pretty close assessment — but not entirely accurate. The Internet has been around for quite a while. It's just that it has been pretty close to dormant for most of its life. In the past, the Internet was the means by which universities and government agencies communicated and transferred information. Now, the Internet is pretty much open to anybody with a computer, a modem, and a phone line. The same can be said for the graphical realm of the Internet — the World Wide Web.

In this part . . .

- ✔ What is the Internet?
- ✔ Why use the Internet?
- ✔ What is the Web?
- ✔ Why do I need the Internet or the Web?

What Is the Internet?

The Internet is a network of computers that extends not only from coast to coast of this country, but around the world as well. Like many of the sprawling, somewhat chaotic technological projects that exist today, the Internet has its origin rooted in the United States Department of Defense. But that was 20 years ago.

Today, the computers that make up the Internet are housed in universities, government agencies, and businesses. In the past, information from these various centers was shared by members of each center. For instance, a professor doing research at a university might have used the Internet to access data from a government agency. While scenarios like the above are still common, now *anyone* and *everyone* is using the Internet to get, and give, all sorts of information from, and to, others.

What Can I Do with the Internet?

An *Internet site* is one of the university, government, or business computers that has opened its resources (or, more likely, some of its resources) to the public. An Internet site usually consists of a powerful computer, such as a mainframe computer, that houses all sorts of files. Using your Macintosh, you'll be able to access these sites and browse through, or download, any number of files. So while your Mac allows you to be a *user of the Internet,* you aren't actually an Internet site — other Internet users won't be able to visit your computer and browse through or copy any of your own files.

In listening to conversations that concern the number of Internet users (Netters), you've no doubt heard all sorts of huge numbers being tossed about: 10 million, 20 million, 30 million or more users. After reading the above paragraph, you now know that these numbers refer to people like yourself — people who access the Internet but don't provide any Internet *content.*

Does this mean that all the talk— and all the books—about the Internet is nothing more than hype? Not at all. In fact, thousands and thousands of Internet sites exist, each teeming with information that's yours for the taking.

✦ Now that you've just found out that you are an Internet *user* rather than a *giver,* you may be inclined to feel guilty about accessing the Net. But wait! Don't feel that you need to spend your time hiding in the dark recesses of the Internet, only occasionally sneaking out to *browse* (read while online) a report or to quickly *download* (copy the file from the Internet to your Mac's hard drive) a file.

✦ Though you can't offer the Internet community the resources that the big guys like universities and businesses can, you, I, and the millions of other Internet users do have something to offer: *information*. Through a variety of means (which just happen to be listed in the next section of this part), the Internet allows people to easily share their knowledge and opinions about any topic imaginable.

What Services Does the Internet Provide?

I've already mentioned that one of your primary uses of the Internet is to access information and files from Internet sites. But there are other uses for this global computer network — and none of them rely on universities, the government, or big business. Instead, the following Internet services rely on the participation of the millions of individuals who access the Internet from their Macs — or PCs.

✦ Worldwide electronic mail — more commonly referred to as e-mail (see Part III)

✦ Mailing lists (see Part IV)

✦ Newsgroups (see Part V)

✦ World Wide Web access (see Part VIII)

✦ Obtaining free files (see Part VI)

✦ Accessing a wealth of data and statistics (see Part VII)

You may have noticed that the World Wide Web appears on the above list. Until recently, creating and placing a *home page* (a private area) on the Web involved a large investment of time and, if the services of a consultant were involved, a large investment of money. Now, both businesses and individuals are finding it relatively painless to stake out their own area on the Web.

Why the Excitement about the World Wide Web?

The World Wide Web (or WWW, or — most commonly — the Web), is a *subset* of the Internet. That is, it is a part of the Web. To become a part of the Web, an Internet site creates its own Web document, or *page*. Any Internet user who has *Web browsing software* (software that allows the information on Web pages to be properly transmitted to your computer) can visit any Web page that isn't password protected. Most Web pages aren't.

✦ Commercial online services such as America Online include such Web browsing software.

✦ As an alternative, you can use Web browsing software that is sold separately from commercial online services. Many browsers are available, with Netscape Navigator being the current rage.

If you have a Web browser, you can use the Web to gain information — information concerning just about anything. The information you find on a Web page may be available elsewhere on the Internet. Or it may not be. Some individuals and businesses distribute their information or files only on Web pages.

Most of the Internet is text-based. When you send e-mail across the Internet, for example, you send a text message — not pictures, or sounds, or digital movies (such as QuickTime movies).

✦ **What makes the Web so special is its graphical nature.** When you visit a Web page, you see text. But you may also encounter any of the multimedia elements (things other than text) just mentioned. Since the Web is a part of the Internet, the Web provides many of the things the Internet provides — but in a more colorful and interesting format. Like "regular" text-based Internet sites, Internet sites that use Web pages can allow visitors to read information or download files.

✦ **Another exciting feature of the Web is *hypertext links*.** Clicking on one of these highlighted words or phrases on a Web page transports you to a different Web page — one that holds information related to the clicked-on link. The Web page that you travel to may be on the same computer as the original Web page, or it may be on a computer across town, or it may even be on a computer half-way around the world. That's possible because the Web is a part of the Internet network — the vast interconnection of computers around the world.

Best of all, the browser software program that you use to traverse the Web keeps track of your trek. So returning to a previously viewed page or returning to the starting point of your journey is fast and simple.

Each day, more and more businesses are creating their own Web pages, so Netters who "surf the Web" (who spend time moving about the various areas of the Internet and Web) can read up on and purchase almost any type of product that they're interested in. If you're on the other side of the business fence, you might consider creating your own Web page and selling your product or products to other Web surfers.

So, just what good is the Web? You've already seen that access to the Web means access to all of the following:

✦ A more colorful, graphical, interesting way of viewing information

✦ Information that might exist nowhere else on the Internet

+ The ability to jump from one area of the Internet to another
+ Documents
+ Pictures
+ Sounds
+ Digital movies

Part II

Getting Started

Getting connected to the Internet, and to the Web in particular, used to be a challenge for even the computer-savvy crowd. Not anymore. Commercial online services make getting connected easy, and local access providers offer an alternative that might save you a few bucks. Whichever direction you go, you of course need a computer and a modem. This part details your choices in each of these areas.

In this part . . .

- ✔ Selecting a Mac for Internet access
- ✔ Choosing the right modem
- ✔ Selecting a commercial online service
- ✔ Selecting a local Internet provider
- ✔ Comparing local Internet providers with commercial services

Hooking Up

To get on the Net you need:

+ A computer

+ A modem

+ A telephone line

+ An Internet service provider

+ Internet access software

Computer requirements

You don't need a Macintosh to access the Internet — I've been told a Windows machine will do the trick in a pinch! You and I know, however, that a Mac makes everything easier and more fun.

All but the lowest-end Macintosh models currently on the market will suffice for getting online. What are the low-end Macs still in production? As of this writing, they are the LC 580 and Performa 475. In general, avoid a Mac that comes with only 4 megabytes of RAM.

If you plan on buying a Mac, here are a few points that may play a part in your decision making:

+ **Memory:** No matter what you intend your Mac to be used for, you can never have too much memory — memory helps program performance. Nowadays, most Macs come with 8 megabytes (MB) of RAM. If you can afford 16MB, take the plunge. If you can't, 8MB will do — but don't get a computer with less than that.

+ **Processor:** You might want a new Power Macintosh, but do you need one? Not for Internet access. The lower-end Performa models are powered by the slower Motorola 68040 processor rather than the faster PowerPC processor, and they still work just fine for going online. If you'd like a Power Mac, get one. But don't base your decision strictly on the fact that you'll be surfin' the Net.

+ **Hard disk:** For Internet access, this part of the Mac is of little concern. The 500MB of hard disk that most Macs come with is more than enough.

+ **Monitor:** This is another topic that is of little concern. A basic 14" or 15" color monitor suffices.

+ **System software:** New Macs come with System 7.5 installed — that works just fine. Any version of System 7 will do, however.

Modem

The link between your Macintosh and an Internet service provider is your *modem*.

✦ The modem is responsible for transmitting data from your Mac to the Internet via the service provider (such as America Online, CompuServe, and so on) and for receiving data from the Internet (again, by way of the service provider).

✦ Modems are inexpensive, so don't try to skimp here — get the fastest that you can afford.

Modem speed is given in *baud rate,* denoted by the acronym *bps* (bits per second). To connect to the Internet:

✦ A baud rate of 28,800 bps is ideal.

✦ A baud rate of 14,400 bps is acceptable. But any speed less will make for time-consuming journeys across the Internet.

In writing and in conversation, Internet surfers generally abbreviate the speed of a modem. A 28,800 baud rate modem may be referred to as a 28.8 modem, or a 28.8K modem (loosely translated, the "K" is an abbreviation for *thousand*, of all things).

In writing, you might see a note saying, "You need a 28.8K modem to really get around the Net." Spoken, that would be, "You need a 28 point 8 *kay* modem to really get around the Net." Likewise, a 14,400 baud rate modem is often simply referred to as a 14.4, or 14.4K, modem.

Telephone line

If your Mac doesn't have an internal modem (a built-in modem), you'll attach an external modem to the modem port on the back of the computer. A *modem port* allows your Macintosh to communicate with your modem. To allow the modem to communicate with the Internet, you attach a standard telephone line to the back of the modem.

You don't *need* to have your local phone company add a second phone line *just* for your Internet use — but you should consider that option. A second line frees up your primary phone line so that people who attempt to contact you by phone can get through. After you discover the simplicity of dialing up the Internet and the variety of information at your disposal once you are connected, you might find yourself spending quite a bit of time surfing the Net. Unfortunately, some people won't be as Internet-proficient as you, and they may still insist on using a phone line for talking!

Service provider

Your Mac communicates with the Internet by dialing the phone number of your Internet access provider. Since your Macintosh isn't an Internet site, it isn't part of the Internet. To access the Net, you need to hook up with a company that *is* an Internet site. There are two types of businesses that are willing to let you use their facilities to jump on the Internet whenever you feel the urge: commercial online services and local Internet providers.

See also "Selecting an Internet Service Provider," later in this part.

Software

To connect to the Internet and to do something once connected, you need software. If you join a commercial online service such as America Online or CompuServe, that service will provide you with a single program capable of performing all the various Internet tasks listed in this section.

If you elect to connect via a local provider, that provider will supply you with the software that you need. Local providers often don't use a single Internet access program — they give you a package that holds several small programs, each tailored for a specific Internet task, such as sending Internet e-mail.

See also "Internet access software," later in this part.

Selecting an Internet Service Provider

To connect to the Internet, your Mac dials the phone number of your Internet access provider. When choosing a provider, you'll be picking from two broad categories: commercial online services and local Internet providers.

Commercial online services

When you become a member of a commercial online service such as America Online, you're paying to use the online services offered by this company. These services include:

✦ Sending e-mail to any other America Online member

✦ "Talking" with other members in chat groups

✦ Downloading files from America Online's vast offerings in its variety of software libraries

One other service that America Online offers is Internet access. When you dial up and connect to America Online, you're just a mouse click or two away from connecting to the Internet. You don't have to worry about *how* America Online connects to the Internet — you just click a button and you, too, are on the Net. While I've used America Online in this example, it isn't the only commercial online service that offers Internet access. All the "biggies" do — including CompuServe, eWorld, and Prodigy.

Local Internet providers

A second means of connecting to the Internet is through a local Internet provider. This type of business doesn't offer any of the services of commercial online services. Instead, a local provider exists simply to be the junction point between the Internet and individuals like yourself — people who have a computer but don't have that computer directly connected to the Internet network.

Local providers versus commercial services

After reading the preceding descriptions, it may seem like commercial online services are always the way to go. After all, you get Internet service *and* a multitude of features unrelated to the Internet. However, the local provider excels in one important area — cost.

Cost

Commercial online services typically bill you by the number of hours you're connected. Local access providers may bill that way, too — or they may not.

✦ A commercial online service charges a fee for each hour that you are connected to the service.

This fee applies whether you're using the online service's features (such as downloading a file from one of its own libraries) or using its interface to the Internet. While the hourly fee isn't exorbitant (typically two to three dollars), if you plan on being connected to the Internet for, say, about an hour a day, your monthly bill can easily exceed fifty dollars.

✦ Local access providers, on the other hand, usually have a couple of different payment plans. Typically, one such plan is for unlimited Internet access for a single set fee — usually about thirty dollars or less.

If you decide to forego a commercial online service and hook up to the Internet via a local access provider, contact the provider that you're interested in and ask if it provides an access number that is in fact local to your area.

✦ Commercial online services all provide local numbers.

From most locations, your modem dials a local phone number in order to connect with the online service.

✦ Local Internet providers are attempting to provide local numbers as well.

The lower membership fees of local providers mean that they haven't installed local access in all major cities, however. If your modem needs to dial an 800 number or a long distance number in order to put you on the Internet, the cost-savings advantage of going with a local Internet provider will be lost.

Internet access software

The following is a list of the major tasks that your Internet access software should be capable of performing:

✦ Connect to an Internet provider

✦ Send and receive e-mail

✦ View messages in newsgroups

✦ Browse the Web

✦ Search for files of interest

✦ Download files of interest

If you access the Internet through a commercial online service, then that service provides you with a single software program that handles all of the preceeding tasks. To perform any of the tasks requires just a mouse click or two, or the typing of a key word.

If you're a member of America Online, for example, you'll use the America Online program to send mail across the Internet. A couple of mouse clicks takes you to an E-Mail Gateway window. From there, you'll click on a small button titled Compose Mail — as shown in the following figure. If you like things simple — as simple as possible — then a commercial online service may be the route for you to take.

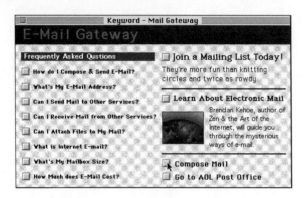

A local Internet provider *may* also give you a single application that performs all of the tasks listed previously. More than likely, though, a local provider will supply a variety of individual programs — each one designed to handle one of the tasks. This multiple-program approach may sound more complicated, but it really isn't because the local provider also supplies you with a program of its own creation — one that "ties together" the individual programs.

The local provider PSINet, for example, supplies you with a program called Internet Valet. By displaying a palette that holds an icon for each of the individually supplied programs, Internet Valet serves as a sort of home base from which you carry out your Internet activities. As shown in this next figure, you send mail across the Internet by first clicking on the palette's mail icon (which runs a mailing program called Eudora) and then selecting New Message from the Message menu.

TIP

If you like the simplicity of a *completely* integrated package, go with the commercial online service. But keep in mind that the local provider's way of doing things does have its advantages:

✦ Each individual program was designed with a singular purpose, so the programs are usually fine-tuned to carry out that one service. That means that the individual programs may do more — and do it quicker — than the software supplied by a commercial online service.

✦ Local Internet providers may allow you to pick from more than one program to perform any one task. For instance, you've probably heard of Netscape's Navigator software. If you want to use this Web browsing software to visit Web pages, you need to have an Internet connection through a local provider — the commercial online services don't let you substitute third-party programs for their own access applications.

Web access

In this book's introduction, I discuss the World Wide Web. Whether you go with an online service or a local provider, you'll have access to this exciting part of the Internet.

✦ Local providers have always included software that provided Web access.

✦ Online services have just recently added Web browsers that enable their members to visit the Web as well.

Some Commercial Online Service Providers

When it comes to simplicity of Internet access, you can't beat a commercial online service. The big-name online services list their memberships in the millions, so you know that they want to do it right. If an online service makes getting on the Internet hard or makes navigating its maze of features difficult, you can bet the technical support service costs would drive the service out of business!

The following sections briefly summarize what the four major online providers offer the Mac community.

America Online

America Online, or AOL, is the fastest growing commercial online service. The popularity of America Online arises from its interface — AOL has always had a true Macintosh interface, with easy point-and-click movement from one area to another. In early 1994, that interface began to extend to Internet access by including an Internet e-mail service. Soon after, newsgroup support and Internet file downloading (FTP) were added. In 1995, a Web browser appeared.

If you've used America Online in the past — when Internet access wasn't included — you have an idea of AOL's Internet interface. America Online has succeeded in smoothly integrating Internet access into its traditional software.

CompuServe

CompuServe is an online service that's been around for quite a while. Even though it has fewer members than AOL, it still has quite a large following — its years of service have ensured that. For most of its life, CompuServe has been text-based. To move from area to area, you would type a number or key word. Now, members have a point-and-click interface much like that of America Online's. The *Mac Compu-Serve Information Manager* (MacCIM) software that's freely distrib-uted by CompuServe makes this type of interface possible. Any CompuServe member — whether a longtime user or newly enrolled — can get a copy of the MacCIM software and start using it to access CompuServe. If you own Web browsing software, MacCIM supports its use. Look for Web support to be fully integrated into MacCIM in 1996.

If you're a subscriber to CompuServe and you're currently accessing CompuServe by means of a text-based program, you should consider downloading a copy of MacCIM from CompuServe — or browsing your supermarket's shelves for a Mac magazine plastic-wrapped with a CompuServe CD-ROM. The free CD-ROM includes a copy of MacCIM.

eWorld

If you purchased your Mac recently, you're probably familiar with Apple's own eWorld online service — it comes bundled with several other programs on many of the new Mac models. Apple's eWorld has a much smaller following than either CompuServe or AOL — it has about one twentieth the number of members as CompuServe does. That, however, is not entirely bad. Since eWorld was created by Apple for Apple users, you know that its content is very Mac-specific. On eWorld, you'll find:

+ Macintosh shareware applications available for download

+ Plenty of live conferences visited by Mac owners

+ A wealth of Apple technical support

Apple started eWorld in mid-1994 and added full Internet access in mid-1995. Using Internet e-mail and performing Internet tasks, such as searching for files and downloading applications, is as easy as carrying out any other task in any other Mac program. For Web access, Apple bought and implemented InterCon's Web Browser —

the same browser used by America Online. To traverse the World Wide Web, you don't need any software other than what you get free from Apple.

If you've heard rumors that eWorld may be folding, you've heard wrong. It will, however, be *changing*. Sometime near mid-1996, it will become Internet-based. By this, Apple means that it intends to create an online community with all the same characteristics currently found on eWorld. The eWorld online service is now a very user-friendly place. The Internet isn't always friendly. Apple hopes to make using the Internet transparent — users of eWorld will still feel as if they're accessing an online service rather than the somewhat chaotic global network of the Internet.

Prodigy

Prodigy is a large online service — it has fewer members than America Online, but about the same membership as CompuServe. Prodigy is a joint venture of Sears and IBM, so it should come as no surprise that a large percentage of Prodigy users access this online service from Windows machines. The Prodigy software that Mac owners use is obviously adapted from the Windows version:

+ Windows don't always have a Mac look to them.

+ Text appears in a Prodigy font that is decidedly different from what Mac users are used to seeing.

+ Navigation often seems clumsy.

Despite its drawbacks, Prodigy does offer full Internet and Web access. If you're already familiar with Prodigy — perhaps you access it from IBM-compatible machines at work or school — you may want to stick with this service rather than learn to work with the software provided by a different commercial online service.

Some Local Internet Access Service Providers

The following list will get you started in your search for a local Internet provider. While the list contains a few of the key players in the local access field, it is not complete. You'll find a more comprehensive list in Chapter 19 of *The Internet For Macs For Dummies*, 2nd Edition.

You can get more facts about these providers by calling or sending each a short e-mail request for information. If you aren't familiar with sending e-mail across the Internet, jump to Part III of this book to get the details!

CRL

This provider has been servicing Mac users for a while now — so you know you'll be able to get technical support if you need any help getting up and running. Like many other providers, CRL is quickly expanding their list of local access numbers. Contact CRL by e-mail at info@crl.com or by voice at 415-381-2800.

IDT

This rapidly expanding Internet service provider offers unlimited Internet access for a flat fee, provides you with a Macintosh version of Navigator Netscape, and is Mac-oriented. Call 800-743-4343 for details.

Pipeline NY

The name doesn't say it all — this one's a little misleading. Pipeline has local access numbers all over the United States. It also has its own Macintosh access software that makes signing up with Pipeline and getting on the Internet very easy. Call 212-267-3636 for more information.

PSINet

This provider has a large number of local access numbers across the country — and the list is growing rapidly. Its Internet Valet software bundles all the individual Mac Internet access programs (including Netscape Navigator) together and makes getting on and using the Internet simple. You can send a short e-mail message to info@psi.com to request details or call 800-774-0852.

Part III

Electronic Mail

Sending electronic mail, or e-mail, may be the first task you attempt when you log on to the Internet. Sending mail that almost instantly reaches a friend, relative, or business a hundred or a thousand miles away provides you with proof that you really are on the Net. In this part, you see that no matter what service provider your Internet account is with, sending and receiving e-mail is easy. For a refresher on service providers, *see* Part II.

In this part . . .

✔ **Finding e-mail addresses**

✔ **Sending e-mail from AOL, CompuServe, Eudora, eWorld, and Prodigy**

✔ **Receiving e-mail from those same services**

✔ **Working with e-mail after you've received it**

✔ **Practicing proper etiquette**

General Internet Addresses

To send e-mail across the Internet, you need the intended recipient's address. An Internet address is composed of three parts:

+ **Mailbox name (user name, screen name, or user ID):** Everything that precedes the @ symbol (explained later) is considered the mailbox name. Mailbox names can include letters and numbers—but not commas, spaces, or parentheses.

Because spaces can't be included, a user who has a screen name of Joe Cat will have a mailbox name of JoeCat.

Capitalization in a mailbox name is unimportant; America Online user Joe Cat can be reached using either `JoeCat@aol.com` or `joecat@aol.com`.

+ **@ (the "at" symbol):** You'll always find the @ symbol separating the mailbox name from the host name.

+ **Host name:** The host name indicates on what system the recipient has his or her account. For example, `joecat@aol.com` is a person with an account on America Online. In this example the host name is `aol.com`.

The last piece of information in the host name is called the *address zone.* Zones that are three characters in length represent an organization. In the "Internet Addresses for Commercial Online Service Users" section, you see that all of the commercial online service addresses end with `com` because they are all commercial organizations (places of business). This table shows the type of organization that the different zones represent.

Zone	*Organization Type*
com	Commercial organization
edu	Educational institution
gov	Government body or department
int	International organization
mil	United States military site
net	Networking organization
org	Organization that doesn't "fit" into any other zone

Internet Addresses for Commercial Online Service Users

If you're sending e-mail to someone with an account on a commercial online service, you need to know that person's user name (screen name) or user ID. In most cases, the user name is followed by the @ symbol, the online service name, and then `.com`. As you can see in the following table, the GEnie service strays from that convention.

Remember: Internet address mailboxes (the first part of the address) cannot include commas or spaces. As a result, a CompuServe address includes a period in place of the comma in a user's ID, and an America Online user name is changed from `John Doe` to `johndoe`.

Service	Typical User Name or ID	Internet Address
America Online	John Doe	johndoe@aol.com
CompuServe	73747,1401	73747.1401@compuserve.com
Delphi	jdoe	jdoe@delphi.com
eWorld	John Doe	johndoe@eworld.com
GEnie	DOE332	DOE332@genie.geis.com
Prodigy	LLDG53A	LLDG53A@prodigy.com

America Online

America Online allows you to send e-mail to other AOL members or to Internet members. The process for doing either is the same — only the address format differs. When sending e-mail to another AOL user, simply use that member's account name (screen name) as the mailing address. When sending e-mail to someone with an Internet account, include the @ symbol and the appropriate suffix `aol.com`. When sending e-mail to a user with an account on a different service, you need to use the correct suffix.

See also "Internet Addresses for Commercial Online Service Users," in this part.

If someone with an Internet account wants to send e-mail to you at your AOL account, that person will need to know your AOL account name. The Internet user should use your AOL account name followed by `@aol.com`. For example, if your AOL account name is `DanParks`, then your Internet address is `DanParks@aol.com`.

TIP

Finding an address

To find the address of another AOL member, follow these steps:

1. Choose Member⇨Member Directory.

The Search Member Directory window appears.

2. Click on Search the Member Directory.

3. Click on the OK button.

4. Type the AOL member's last name.

5. Click on the Search button.

The screen names of all AOL members that have the name you typed appear at the bottom of the window.

Sending mail

1. Choose Mail⇨Compose Mail.

An untitled Compose Mail window appears.

2. Type the recipient's address in the To box.

3. If you want others to receive this same message, type their addresses in the cc box.

4. Type a descriptive message title in the Subject box.

5. Type your message in the window's main box — the largest box in the window.

If you've previously copied text from another message or another document (by choosing Edit⇨Copy), you can paste that text in the main box (by choosing Edit⇨Paste).

6. Click on the Send Now icon.

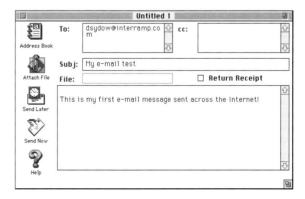

Reading new mail

1. Choose Mail⇨Read New Mail.

   The New Mail window appears with a list of all new mail messages in it.

2. Double-click on the message of interest.

   The new message appears in its own window.

3. If other new messages are present, click on the Next arrow to read the next one.

Replying to new mail

1. When you are finished reading a message, click on the Reply icon in the window that is displaying the read message.

   An untitled Compose Mail window appears with the To box and the Subject box appropriately filled in. You can highlight the text in the Subject box and then type in a new subject if you prefer.

2. Type or paste your message in the window's main box — the largest box in the window.

3. When you are done, click on the Send Now icon.

Forwarding mail to someone else

1. When you are finished reading a message, click on the Forward icon in the window that is displaying the read message.

   An untitled Forward Mail window appears with the Subject box appropriately filled in. You can edit the words in the Subject box if you wish.

2. Type the recipient's address in the To box.

3. Type a comment, if you like, in the Forward Comment box.

4. When you are done, click on the Send Now icon.

Saving read mail

1. Display the message to save by following the steps in the "Reading new mail" section.

2. Choose File⇨Save As.

A standard Save File window appears.

3. Enter the file name that you want to save this message as — you can type in any name you want, up to 32 characters in length.

4. Click on either the Mail Read icon or the Text icon to establish the format of the saved file (you have the option of saving the file as a mail file rather than a text file that can be read by word processors).

5. Click on the pop-up menu at the top of the window if you want to select a different folder to put the file in. You can also double-click on folders in the window's list to establish which folder the file ends up in.

6. Click on the Save button to save the message to a file.

Reading saved mail

1. Choose File⇨Open.

A standard Open File window appears.

2. Use the pop-up menu to move to the folder that holds the mail file.

3. Double-click on the name of the file to open it.

CompuServe

CompuServe allows you to send e-mail to other CompuServe members or to Internet members. The process for doing either is the same — only the address format differs. When sending e-mail to another CompuServe user, use that member's CompuServe ID as the mailing address.

When sending e-mail to someone with an Internet account, you must precede the user's address with the word INTERNET followed by a colon. The word *INTERNET* may be typed in uppercase or lowercase letters. That is, capitalization is optional. As an example, if you're using your CompuServe account to send e-mail to an America Online user who has a screen name of DanParks, the address you'd use is

INTERNET:danparks@aol.com. If you forget the INTERNET: part,
CompuServe will *not* send the message and will display a window
telling you so. When sending e-mail to a user with an account on a
different service, you need to use the correct suffix — *see* the
"Internet Addresses for Commercial Online Service Users" section in
this part.

If someone with an Internet account wants to send e-mail to you at
your CompuServe account, he or she will need to know your
CompuServe ID. That person should use your ID followed by
@compuserve.com.

One important thing for the Internet user to be aware of is that the
comma in your ID must be changed to a period when mail is being
sent to you across the Internet. For example, if your CompuServe ID is
73747,1401, then your Internet address is 73747.1401@aol.com.

Finding an address

To find the address of another CompuServe member, follow these
steps:

> *1.* Choose Mail⇨Member Directory.
>
> The Member Directory Search window appears.
>
> *2.* Type the last name of the member to search for.
>
> *3.* Click on the Add button.
>
> *4.* Click on the Search button.

The Address of all CompuServe members with names that match the
one you typed will appear at the bottom of the window.

Sending mail

> *1.* Choose Mail⇨Create Mail.
>
> A Creating Mail window appears.

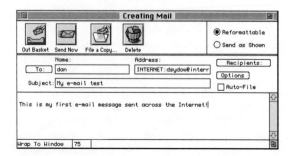

2. Type the recipient's name in the Name box.

3. Type the recipient's address in the Address box.

4. If you want another person to receive this same message, click on the Recipients button. Type that person's name and address in the Name and Address boxes, click on the Cc:>> button, and then click on the Done button. You'll then be back at the Creating Mail window.

5. Type a descriptive message title in the Subject box.

6. Type or paste your message in the window's main box.

7. When you are finished, click on the Send Now icon.

Reading new mail offline

CompuServe makes it easy for you to get all your new mail online and then read it offline — saving you online charges while you read. To read mail offline, first connect with CompuServe as you always do and then follow these steps:

1. Choose Mail⇨Send & Receive All Mail.

   A Send All Mail Status window indicating message retrieval progress appears.

2. Click on the OK button when the message or messages have been retrieved.

3. Choose File⇨Disconnect.

4. Choose Mail⇨In Basket.

5. Double-click on the message that you want to read.

   The new message appears in its own window.

Reading new mail online

1. Click on the Mail icon on the icon bar.

   A window listing your new messages appears.

2. Double-click on the message that you want to read.

   The new message appears in its own window — as shown in the following figure.

Replying to new mail

1. When you are finished reading a message, click on the Reply icon in the window that is displaying the read message.

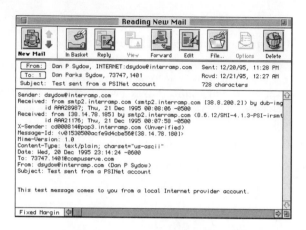

A Reply window appears with the Name box, Address box, and the Subject box appropriately filled in. You can highlight the words in the Subject box and type in a new subject if you wish.

2. Type your message in the window's main box — the largest box in the window.

If appropriate, you can copy text from another mail message or another type of document (choose File⇨Copy) and then paste that text in the window's main box (choose File⇨Paste).

3. When you are finished, click on the Send Now icon.

Forwarding mail to someone else

1. When you are finished reading a message, click on the Forward icon in the window that is displaying the read message.

A Forwarding window appears with the Subject box appropriately filled in. You can edit the words in the Subject box if you wish.

2. Type the recipient's name in the Name box.

3. Type the recipient's address in the Address box.

4. Type a comment, if you like, above the text that appears in the main box.

5. When you are finished, click on the Send Now icon.

Saving read mail

The Filing Cabinet is a folder on your hard disk where MacCIM stores your e-mail messages and other files that you want saved. To store an e-mail message in the Filing Cabinet:

1. Display the message to save by following the steps in the "Reading new mail online" or "Reading new mail offline" section.

2. Click on the File icon.

The Filing Cabinet window appears.

3. Click on the New Folder button if you wish to create an appropriately named subdirectory (folder) in which to save this message.

4. Click on the Save button to save the message.

Reading saved mail

The Filing Cabinet is a folder that holds your saved e-mail messages. To read a message that you've previously saved in the Filing Cabinet:

1. Choose Mail⇨Filing Cabinet.

The Filing Cabinet window appears.

2. Double-click on the name of the e-mail message to read.

Eudora

Eudora allows you to easily send e-mail to Internet members. If you're sending e-mail to members of a commercial online service such as America Online or CompuServe, *see* the appropriate style of e-mail address discussed in the "Internet Addresses for Commercial Online Service Users" section in this part.

If someone with an Internet account wants to send e-mail to you, that person will need to know your account name. When you subscribed to your local Internet service provider, that provider sent you documentation that included your e-mail address — refer to those papers now.

Sending mail

1. Choose Message⇨New Message.

An untitled new mail window appears.

2. Type the recipient's address following the word *To*.

3. If you want others to receive this same message, type their addresses following the letters *Cc*.

4. Type a descriptive message title following the word *Subject*.

5. Type or paste your message in the bottom of the window.

6. When you are done, click on the Send button.

Reading new mail

1. Choose File⇨Check Mail.

   The first time that you check mail during each session with Eudora, a Password window appears.

2. Enter your e-mail account password.

   Your e-mail account password is usually the same as the password that your local Internet provider issued to you — the password you may be required to enter when you connect to the Internet.

   You can avoid having to enter the password by telling Eudora to remember it. *See also* the "Saving your e-mail account password" section.

3. Click on the OK button.

   If you have new mail, Eudora will display a window telling you so.

4. Click on the OK button.

   The In mailbox appears.

5. Double-click on the message to be read.

   The new message appears in its own window.

The following figure shows an example of a mail message being read in Eudora. Note that the window's title holds the address of the sender of the message — in this example the message is from an account with Apple's online service eWorld.

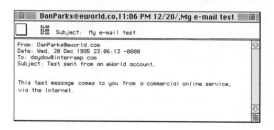

You can avoid having to check for new mail by telling Eudora to automatically check for new messages — *see* the "Automatically checking messages" section.

Saving your e-mail account password

By telling Eudora to remember your password, you can avoid having to enter it each time you check your mail.

1. Choose Special⇨Settings.

The Settings window appears.

2. Click on the Checking Mail icon.

3. Check the Save password check box.

4. Click on the OK button.

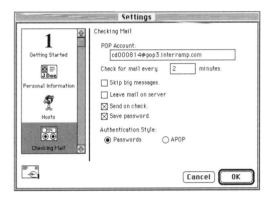

Automatically checking messages

You can avoid having to check for new mail by telling Eudora to automatically check for new messages — even when Eudora is running in the background.

1. Choose Special⇨Settings.

The Settings window appears.

2. Click the Checking Mail icon.

3. Enter a number in the Check for mail every box.

4. Click on the OK button.

If new mail arrives during your session, Eudora will let you know.

Replying to new mail

1. When you are finished reading a message, choose Message⇨Reply.

A Reply window appears with the To box and the Subject box appropriately filled in. You can edit the words in the Subject box if you wish.

2. Type your message in the window's main box — the largest box in the window. If appropriate, you can copy text from another mail message or another type of document (choose File⇨Copy) and then paste that text in the window's main box (choose File⇨Paste).

3. When you are done, click on the Send button.

Forwarding mail to someone else

1. When you are finished reading a message, choose Message⇨Forward.

A Forward window appears with the Subject box appropriately filled in. You can edit the words in the Subject box if you wish.

2. Type the recipient's address in the To box.

3. Type any additional text, if you like, in the main box.

4. When you are done, click on the Send button.

Saving read mail

1. Display the message to save.

2. Choose File⇨Save As.

A standard Save File window appears.

3. Enter the file name that you want to save this message as.

4. Click on the pop-up menu at the top of the window if you want to select a different folder into which the file should go. You can also double-click on folders in the window's list to establish which folder the file ends up in.

5. Click on the Save button to save the message to a file.

Reading saved mail

1. Choose File⇨Open.

A standard Open File window appears.

2. Use the pop-up menu at the top of the Open File window and the list in the contents of the window to open the folder that holds the mail file.

3. Double-click on the name of the file to open.

eWorld

If you have an eWorld account, you can send e-mail to other eWorld members or to Internet members. The process for doing either is similar — only the address format differs. When sending e-mail to another eWorld user, just use that member's account name (screen name) as the mailing address. When sending e-mail to someone with an Internet account, include the @ symbol and the appropriate suffix — refer back to the "Internet Addresses for Commercial Online Service Users" section in this part.

If someone with an Internet account wants to send e-mail to you at your eWorld account, that person needs to know your eWorld screen name. The Internet user then uses your eWorld screen name followed by @eworld.com. For example, if your eWorld account name is DanParks, then your Internet address is DanParks@eworld.com.

Finding an address

To find the address of another eWorld member, follow these steps:

1. Choose Membership⇨Member Directory.

The Member Director window appears.

2. Type the eWorld member's last name.

3. Click on the Find button.

Sending mail

1. Choose eMail⇨Compose New Message.

A Compose New Message window appears.

2. Type the recipient's address in the To box.

3. If you want others to receive this same message, type their addresses in the cc box.

4. Type a descriptive message title in the Subject box.

5. Type your message in the window's main box — the largest box in the window. If you've previously copied text from another message or another document (by choosing Edit⇨Copy), you can paste that text in the main box (by choosing Edit⇨Paste).

6. When you are done, click on the Send Now button.

Reading new mail

1. Choose eMail⇨Unopened Mail.

   The Unopened Mail window appears.

2. Double-click on the message to be read.

   The new message appears in its own window.

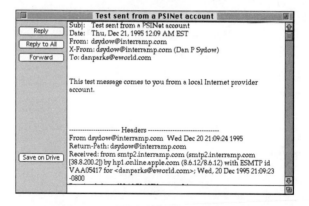

3. If other new messages are present, click on the Next arrow to read the next one.

Replying to new mail

1. When you are finished reading a message, click on the Reply button in the window that is displaying the read message.

   A Compose New Message window appears with the To box and the Subject box appropriately filled in. You can edit the words in the Subject box if you wish.

2. Type your message in the window's main box — the largest box in the window. If you've previously copied text from another message or another document (by choosing Edit⇨Copy), you can paste that text in the main box (by choosing Edit⇨Paste).

3. When you are done, click on the Send Now button.

Forwarding mail to someone else

1. When you are finished reading a message, click on the Forward button in the window that is displaying the read message.

   An untitled Forward Mail window appears with the Subject box appropriately filled in. You can edit the words in the Subject box if you wish.

2. Type the recipient's address in the To box.

3. Type a comment, if you like, in the main box.

4. When you are done, click on the Send Now button.

Saving read mail

1. Display the message to save.

2. Click on the Save on Drive button.

The eWorld software saves your read message in a folder that has your screen name in its title. This folder is found in the eWorld Mail folder, which itself is located in the main eWorld folder — the folder that holds the eWorld program.

Reading saved mail

1. Choose File⇨Open.

   A standard Open File window appears.

2. Use the pop-up menu at the top of the window to move to the folder that holds the mail file.

3. Double-click on the name of the file to open.

Prodigy

From a Prodigy account you can send e-mail to other Prodigy members or to Internet members. When sending e-mail to another Prodigy user, just use that member's account ID as the mailing address. When sending e-mail to someone with an Internet account, include the @ symbol and the appropriate suffix — refer back to the "Internet Addresses for Commercial Online Service Users" section in this part.

If someone with an Internet account wants to send e-mail to you at your Prodigy account, that person needs to know your Prodigy ID. The Internet user uses your Prodigy ID followed by @prodigy.com. For example, if your Prodigy ID is LLDG53A, then your Internet address is LLDG53A@prodigy.com.

While Prodigy software does supply users with a graphical interface, its look and feel is decidedly "unMacintosh." Prodigy is working on revising its access software, so be forewarned that some of the steps listed on the following pages are subject to change.

As mentioned in the "Prodigy" section of Part II, Prodigy is a joint venture between Sears and IBM — which should explain why the software interface doesn't have a Macintosh look-and-feel.

Finding an address

To find the address of another Prodigy member, follow these steps:

1. Choose Jump⇨Jump To.

2. Type **member list** in the Jump box.

3. Click on the OK button.

   The Member List window appears.

4. Click on the By Name button under the word *Search*.

   The Name Entry window appears.

5. Type the Prodigy member's last name (or a part of the name) and then press the Return key.

6. Type the Prodigy member's first name (or a part of the name) and then press the Return key.

   You may type up to 28 characters in either of the name boxes.

7. Click on the OK button.

   The State/Province Selection window appears.

8. Click on SEARCH ALL.

Sending mail to one recipient

1. Choose Jump⇨Jump To.

2. Type **mail** in the Jump box.

3. Click the OK button.

   The Mailbox window appears.

4. Click on the Write button.

A Write window appears.

5. Type the recipient's address in the To box.

If you want others to receive this same message, *see* the "Sending mail to multiple recipients" section.

6. Type a descriptive message title in the Subject box.

7. Type your message in the window's main box — the largest box in the window. If you've previously copied text from another message or another document (by choosing Edit⇨Copy), you can paste that text in the main box (by choosing Edit⇨Paste).

8. When you are finished, click on the Send button.

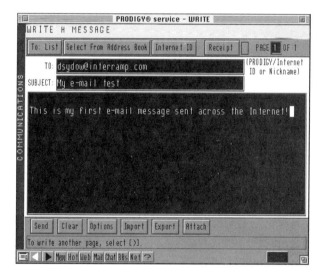

Sending mail to multiple recipients

If you want others to receive this same message, perform the following steps:

1. Choose Jump⇨Jump To.

2. Type **mail** in the Jump box.

3. Click the OK button.

The Mailbox window appears.

4. Click on the Write button.

A Write window appears.

5. Click on the To: List button.

6. Type the person's address in the To box.

7. Press the Return key.

8. Enter another address if desired.

9. Click on the OK button when you are finished.

10. Type a descriptive message title in the Subject box.

11. Type your message in the window's main box — the largest box in the window. If you've previously copied text from another message or another document (by choosing Edit⇨Copy), you can paste that text in the main box (by choosing Edit⇨Paste).

12. When you are finished, click on the Send button.

Reading new mail

1. Choose Jump⇨Jump To.

2. Type **mail** in the Jump box.

3. Click on the OK button.

The Mailbox window appears.

4. Click on the numbered box that appears to the left of the message to be read.

The new message appears in its own window.

5. If other new messages are present, click on the Next button to read the next one.

Replying to new mail

1. When you are finished reading a message, click on the Reply button in the window that is displaying the read message.

A new Write A Reply window appears with the To box and the Subject box appropriately filled in. You can edit the words in the Subject box if you wish.

2. Type your message in the window's main box — the largest box in the window. If appropriate, you can copy text from another mail message or another type of document (choose File⇨Copy) and then paste that text in the window's main box (choose File⇨Paste).

3. When you are done, click on the Send button.

Forwarding mail to someone else

1. When you are finished reading a message, click on the Forward button in the window that is displaying the read message.

A new Forward A Message window appears with the Subject box appropriately filled in. You can edit the words in the Subject box if you wish.

2. Type the recipient's address in the To box.

3. Type a comment, if you like, in the main box.

4. When you are done, click on the Send button.

Saving read mail

1. Display the message to save.

See also the "Reading new mail" section for the steps necessary to read a new message.

2. Click on the Download button.

The Download window appears.

3. In the File box, type the name to be given to the saved message.

4. Click on the Begin Download button.

The Prodigy software saves your read message in the main Prodigy folder — the folder that holds the Prodigy program.

Proper E-Mail Etiquette

E-mail sent across the Internet is uncensored, which means all Netters are trusted to regulate themselves. Although no hard and fast rules exist when sending e-mail, you can't go wrong living by the golden rule. In addition, each user is encouraged to abide by the following civilities:

+ **Don't flame.** *Flaming* is a venting of your outrage or frustration at something. The recipient of your mail has probably had a hard day, too — don't take things out on him or her.

+ **Avoid swearing or obnoxious language.**

+ **Don't use all uppercase in a message.** IT LOOKS LIKE YOU'RE SHOUTING AT THE RECIPIENT.

+ **Be careful with sarcasm.** The written word can be easily misinterpreted. What you meant as humor may be perceived as nastiness. When you do use sarcasm, follow the sentence with a smiley :-) or a winking smiley ;-) to let the recipient know your intentions.

Part IV

Mailing Lists

When you send an e-mail message, it generally goes to one recipient. To allow you to send the same message to a few people, mailing systems let you "cc," or carbon copy, the message by specifying more than one recipient address.

But consider this scenario: You want to find and then communicate with a large number of people who share a common interest — whether that interest is vintage automobiles, breeding parakeets, or collecting stamps. How do you go about easily sending a single e-mail message to perhaps a dozen, a hundred, or a thousand or more people? And how do you make it possible for e-mail sent by any of the other members of this common-interest group to reach your mailbox? The answer is, of course, by using a mailing list.

A *mailing list* is a usually automated service that you subscribe to. Once you subscribe, a copy of an e-mail message sent by *any* one mailing list member automatically is delivered to your address. And any e-mail message that you send to the mailing list reaches all other members. A mailing list thus enables you to participate in conversations of interest with any number of people.

In this part . . .

- ✔ Addresses used with mailing lists
- ✔ Find a mailing list of interest to you
- ✔ Subscribing to a mailing list from AOL, CompuServe, Eudora, eWorld, and Prodigy
- ✔ Receiving mail from mailing list members
- ✔ Sending mail to mailing list members
- ✔ Unsubscribing from a mailing list

About Mailing Lists

Each mailing list has two Internet e-mail addresses:

✦ **List address:** You use the list address anytime that you want to send e-mail to other list members. Sending a single e-mail message to the list address results in your message going to every list member — whether the list has ten or ten thousand people subscribed to it.

✦ **Administrative address:** You use the administrative address only when sending commands to the list administrator — the overseer of the list.

Typically, you only use this address to subscribe and unsubscribe to a list. A message sent to this address is received by only one recipient — the administrator of the list. That makes good sense — there's no point in sending an e-mail message to every other member just to say, "I'm dropping off this list."

While the particulars of working with mailing lists vary from online service to online service, several commonalities exist — as described here.

Receiving mail from a list

After you have subscribed to a mailing list, you don't need to do anything special to receive mail from the other members of the list — mail automatically appears in your e-mail mailbox.

Sending mail to a list

After subscribing to a mailing list, you can send e-mail to other list members at any time. Make sure that the recipient's address is the list address (*not* the list's *administrative address*). Then compose and send your message as you would any other Internet e-mail message. If you need to brush up on how to send e-mail, ***see also*** Part III.

Subscribing to a list

To subscribe to a mailing list:

1. Find the list's administrative address.

• Some commercial online services allow you to easily search for mailing list names that match your interests, and the information that accompanies the name tells you the address of the list's administrator. Usually, you find Listproc or LISTSERV in the address.

- Other online services and local Internet access services don't make it quite as easy to find lists. The best way to find out what mailing lists are available is to connect to the World Wide Web and use your Web browser to connect to URL http://www.neosoft.com/internet/paml. If that last sentence looks like nothing but gibberish, you need to read about the Web in Part VIII!

2. Create an e-mail message to send to the list's administrator.

3. Fill in the address, subject, and body of the message as instructed in the information that you received from your mailing list search in step 1.

4. Send the e-mail message.

   The administrator replies by sending you an e-mail message confirming your request. This message usually includes the list address. Make note of that address so that you can send e-mail to list participants.

See also the appropriate commercial online service name in this part for more information on subscribing to a list.

Unsubscribing to a list

To *unsubscribe,* or quit a list, send an unsubscribe e-mail message to the list's administrative address. ***Remember:*** When you initially searched for the mailing list, instructions were provided on just what this unsubscribe message should contain.

If you've been on a list awhile and you don't know how to get off the list, search for the list's instructions.

See also the appropriate commercial online service name in this part for more information on unsubscribing to a list.

America Online

AOL and eWorld are the commercial online services that provide members with an easy way to search for mailings lists — as you'll see in the "Finding a particular list" section below. After you find a list of interest, become a member by sending a subscribe message to the list's administrative address.

Finding a particular list

1. Choose Go To➪Keyword.

   The Keyword window appears.

2. Type **mailing lists**.

3. Click on the Go button.

The Mailing Lists window appears.

4. Click on the small box labeled *Search the Database*.

The Internet Mailing Lists search window appears.

5. Type a word or words that describe the topic of interest.

6. Click on the List Articles button.

7. Double-click on the mailing list name of interest.

A window with a list description and subscribing/unsubscribing information opens. To subscribe to the list, follow the instructions in the window.

See also "Subscribing to a list," in this section.

Subscribing to a list

1. Select Mail⇨Compose Mail.

A new, empty Compose Mail window appears.

2. Fill in the Address, Subject, and main boxes as instructed in the text file that holds information about the list.

See also "Finding a particular list," in this section.

The following figure shows the results of an AOL search for mailing lists dealing with health care reform. In this figure, the front-most window shows the instructions to subscribe and unsubscribe to one mailing list.

The window in the background shows an AOL e-mail message filled out and ready to be sent to the administrative address. Since the subscription instructions say nothing about the e-mail subject, you can assume that the contents of the Subject field are unimportant.

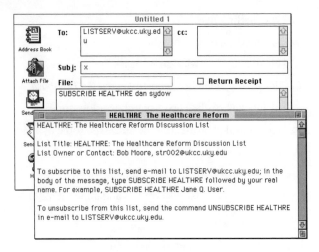

3. Send the e-mail message.

Shortly after sending an e-mail message to a list's administrative address, you'll receive an e-mail reply confirming your request. This reply will include the list address itself. Make note of this address — you'll need it if you want to send e-mail to the other members of the list.

You can see in the next figure that the reply sent by the administrator of the health care reform mailing list includes both:

- The administrator address (LISTSERV@UKCC.UKY.EDU)

- The list address (HEALTHRE@UKCC.UKY.EDU)

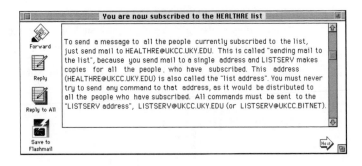

Unsubscribing to a list

To remove yourself from a mailing list, send an unsubscribe e-mail message to the list's administrative address. **Remember:** When you initially searched for the list, instructions were provided on just what this unsubscribe message should contain.

See also "Finding a particular list," in this section.

The figure shows an unsubscribe e-mail message.

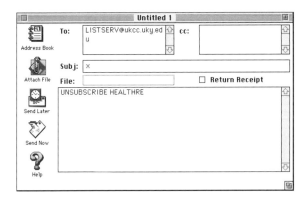

CompuServe

Some commercial online services use a point-and-click interface to make browsing for a mailing list that matches your interests easy. CompuServe isn't such an online service.

To find a mailing list, your best bet is to access the Web — Part VIII tells you all about accessing the Web. After you've subscribed to a mailing list, you can use your CompuServe account for mailing list participation — new messages from list members automatically appear in your mailbox.

Finding a particular list

1. From your Web browser, go to page
http://www.neosoft.com/internet/paml.

This page is a large directory of mailing lists — a list of lists. The list is maintained by Stephanie da Silva, who updates it monthly.

See also Part VIII for information on the Web.

2. Click on one of the topics in the page's index feature to search for a topic of interest.

3. After you find a topic, take note of the instructions for subscribing and unsubscribing to the list.

Subscribing to a list

1. Select Mail⇨Create Mail.

A new, empty Creating Mail window appears.

2. Fill in the Address, Subject, and main boxes as instructed in the text file that holds information about the list (*see* the "Finding a particular list" section).

3. Click on the Send Now icon.

In a short time you'll receive e-mail notifying you that you've been added to the mailing list. Take note of the address that is to be used if you wish to send e-mail to all other members of the list.

Unsubscribing to a list

To unsubscribe to a list, simply send an unsubscribe e-mail message to the list's administrative address. ***Remember:*** When you initially joined the mailing list, instructions were provided on what this unsubscribe message should contain.

See also "Finding a particular list," in this section.

Eudora

If you access the Internet through the use of a local access provider, you'll use the electronic mail program supplied by that provider to work with mailing lists.

Before joining a list, though, you need to find the name and administrative address of a list that matches your interest. To find the name and address, use the Web browser (such as Netscape Navigator) that is a part of your access software package.

See also Part VIII for descriptions of accessing the Web and Netscape Navigator.

Finding a particular list

1. From your Web browser, go to page
http://www.neosoft.com/internet/paml.

This page is a large directory of mailing lists — a list of lists. The list is maintained by Stephanie da Silva, who updates it monthly

See also Part VIII for information on the Web.

2. Click on one of the topics in the page's index feature to search for a topic of interest.

3. After you find a topic, take note of the instructions for subscribing and unsubscribing to the list.

Subscribing to a list

1. Choose Message⇨New Message.

An untitled Compose Mail window appears.

2. Fill in the To, Subject, and main boxes as instructed in the text file that holds information about the list (***see*** the "Finding a particular list" section).

3. When you are finished, click on the Send icon.

Soon you'll receive e-mail notifying you that you've been added to the mailing list. Make a note of the address that is to be used when sending e-mail to all other members of the list.

Unsubscribing to a list

To unsubscribe to a list, send an unsubscribe e-mail message to the list's administrative address. When you initially searched for the mailing list, instructions were provided on what this unsubscribe message should contain

eWorld

eWorld and AOL are the commercial online services that make working with mailing lists a breeze. Both services provide a simple-to-use search facility that allows you to easily find a mailing list for the topic that suits your interest — as you see in the "Finding a particular list" section.

Finding a particular list

1. Click on the Internet On-Ramp area of the introductory screen — referred to as the Town Square screen. (If this window isn't open, choose Places⇨Town Square.)

The eWorld Internet window appears. From here, you'll be able to move to the mailing list area of the Internet.

2. Click on the Mail Subscriptions (Internet Mailing Lists) icon.

The Internet Mailing Lists window appears.

3. Double-click on the folder that you are interested in.

4. Continue double-clicking on folders until you reach a window that holds list names.

5. Double-click on the list of interest.

A window with a list description and subscribing/unsubscribing information opens. To subscribe to the list, follow the instructions in the window.

See also "Subscribing to a list," in this section.

If you know the topic you want to subscribe to:

1. Click on the Find icon in the Internet Mailing Lists window.

2. Enter the topic — you can type in more than one word.

3. Then click on the Find button.

Subscribing to a list

1. Select eMail⇨Compose New Message.

A new, empty Compose New Mail window appears.

2. Fill in the To address, the Subject, and main boxes as instructed in the text file that holds information about the list (***see*** the "Finding a particular list" section).

The following figure shows the results of an eWorld search for mailing lists dealing with health care reform. The front-most window in the figure shows the instructions to subscribe and unsubscribe to one mailing list that deals with this topic.

The window in the background shows an eWorld e-mail message filled out and ready to be sent to the list's administrative address.

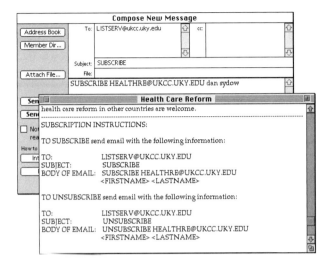

3. Click on the Send Now button.

After sending an e-mail message to a list's administrative address, the administrator replies by sending you an e-mail message confirming your request — the next figure shows such a reply. The message sent to you should include the list address. Make note of this address so that you can send e-mail to list participants.

Notice in the figure that the reply sent by the health care reform mailing list administrator includes both

- The administrator address (LISTSERV@UKCC.UKY.EDU)

- The list address (HEALTHRE@UKCC.UKY.EDU)

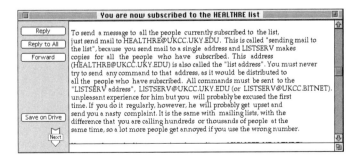

Unsubscribing to a list

To unsubscribe to a list, send an unsubscribe e-mail message to the list's administrative address. **Remember:** When you initially searched for the mailing list, you received instructions on just what this unsubscribe message should contain.

See also "Finding a particular list," in this section.

The figure shows a typical unsubscribe e-mail message.

Prodigy

Like CompuServe, Prodigy doesn't provide a simple means for finding mailing lists of interest — you'll probably want to use Prodigy's Web browser to locate a list that interests you.

See also Part VIII for a discussion on Prodigy's Web browser.

After you subscribe to a mailing list, though, you can use your Prodigy account for mailing list participation. Any e-mail messages sent by other list members will automatically show up in your mailbox.

Finding a particular list

1. From the Prodigy Web browser, go to page
   http://www.neosoft.com/internet/paml.

   This page is a list of lists. That is, it consists of a directory of mailing lists. The list is maintained and updated by Stephanie da Silva.

See also Part VIII for information on the Web.

2. Click on one of the topics in the page's index feature to search for a topic of interest.

3. After you find a topic, take note of the instructions for subscribing and unsubscribing to the list.

Subscribing to a list

1. Choose Jump⇨Jump To.

2. Type **mail** in the Jump box.

3. Click on the OK button.

The Mailbox window appears.

4. Click on the Write button.

A Write window appears.

5. Fill in the To, Subject, and main boxes as instructed in the text file.

6. Click on the Send icon.

In a short time, you'll receive e-mail notifying you that you've been added to the mailing list. Take note of the address that is to be used if you wish to send e-mail to all other members of the list.

Unsubscribing to a list

To unsubscribe to a list, send an unsubscribe e-mail message to the list's administrative address. ***Remember:*** When you initially searched for the mailing list, instructions were provided on what this unsubscribe message should contain.

See also "Finding a particular list," in this section.

Part V

Newsgroups

Usenet newsgroups (also referred to as newsgroups or
Net news) are similar to the topic of Part IV — mailing
lists. Recall that a mailing list consists of a group of
people who have an interest in the same topic.
Newsgroups are similar to mailing lists in that each
group is dedicated to a single topic. The difference,
though, is that you don't *belong* to a newsgroup as you
would a mailing list. Instead, you just "pop in" on a
newsgroup when the urge sets in.

You visit a newsgroup and browse through the messages, or articles, posted by other Netters. If you have a
question, or feel inclined to respond to someone else's
question, you post a message of your own to the
newsgroup. With a newsgroup, information isn't ex-
changed by e-mail, as it is for a mailing list. Instead, you
post your message to a *bulletin board* that is accessible
worldwide.

In this part . . .

- ✓ Newsgroup etiquette

- ✓ Reading newsgroup messages from AOL,
  CompuServe, eWorld, NewsWatcher, and
  Prodigy

- ✓ Replying to a newsgroup message from those
  same services

- ✓ Starting a new topic in a newsgroup from
  those same services

About Newsgroup Names

Like Internet e-mail addresses (*see also* Part III of this book), Usenet newsgroup names consist of parts separated by dots. A couple of examples of newsgroup names are soc.culture.usa and sci.chemistry. While your first exposure to newsgroup names can be disconcerting, further examination reveals that there is an easily understandable logic to the names.

A name starts with the most general area that the newsgroup covers and moves toward the specific. For example, soc.culture.usa is a newsgroup that deals with a social interest (soc). Specifically, that interest is culture (culture). More specifically, the culture is that of the United States (usa). Of course, to be able to decipher a newsgroup name, you need to be familiar with the common abbreviations used in the names. The following table helps out in that respect. Notice that, as these abbreviations describe general categories, you always find them at the start of a newsgroup name.

Newsgroup Abbreviation	*Description*
alt	An "alternative" to the following seven primary newsgroup categories; *alternative* doesn't always mean strange or off-the-wall — but often it does.
comp	Computer-related topics; often quite sophisticated in content.
misc	Miscellaneous topics.
news	Not world news, but newsgroup news; newsgroup announcements may be of interest to some — but not too many — Netters.
rec	Recreational newsgroups; fun topics such as arts, hobbies, and sports.
sci	Science topics; like the comp newsgroups, sci groups are sometimes intense.
soc	Social interest topics; might be sociology or just socializing.
talk	Political, religious, you name it — whatever the topic, you find plenty of sermonizing and arguments here.

Unsurprisingly, newsgroup names that are similar have to do with similar topics — that's the whole idea of using standard abbreviations in newsgroup names. For example, the rec.arts.movies.people newsgroup exists for people to generate discussions about Hollywood and actors, while the rec.arts.movies.reviews newsgroup holds reviews about movies.

thread see p. 77

America Online

America Online makes it easy to follow — and participate in — the goings-on in newsgroups. Read the section, "Starting the AOL newsreader," first. Follow the steps in that section to get to the Newsgroups window. From this "home base" (shown in the figure), you can perform all your newsgroup tasks.

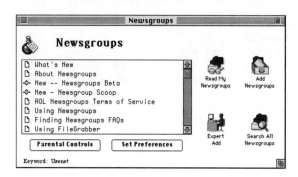

Starting the AOL newsreader

1. Choose Go To⇨Keyword.

The Keyword window appears.

2. Type **newsgroups**.

3. Click on the Go button.

The Newsgroups window appears.

Moving to a newsgroup

Before reading articles, you have to move to a particular newsgroup.

1. Click on the Add Newsgroups icon in the Newsgroups window.

See also "Starting the AOL newsreader," in this section.

A window that holds a hierarchical list of all the newsgroups appears. A *hierarchy* exists to organize the groups. (For example, all groups beginning with alt are bunched together; all groups beginning with rec are together; and so on.)

2. Double-click on one of the hierarchies to see a list of the newsgroups in that hierarchy.

Subhierarchies may be within a hierarchy. If that's the case, continue double-clicking until you reach a list of newsgroups.

3. After finding a newsgroup of interest, double-click on the newsgroup name.

A window holding a list of articles in that newsgroup appears.

Reading a newsgroup article

1. After moving to a newsgroup, double-click on a *thread* (a topic) name within the newsgroup list of articles.

See also "Moving to a newsgroup," in this section.

A window appears holding the text of the first message in the thread.

2. Read the first article in the thread.

3. If more articles are in the same thread, click on the Next Message button to read the next article.

To read an article in a group you're subscribed to, see the "Reading a subscribed newsgroup article" section.

Saving a newsgroup article

If you want to be able to refer back to an article of interest, choose File⇨Save As while the article is in the front-most window. That saves the article as a text file.

Subscribing to a newsgroup

Instead of searching out and moving to one particular newsgroup each time that you want to read that group's messages, find the group one time and then subscribe to it. Subscribing to a newsgroup also allows you to reply to messages posted by others. AOL allows you to subscribe to any number of newsgroups.

All subscribed groups are easily accessible from the Newsgroups window by clicking the Read My Newsgroups button. *See also* "Starting the AOL newsreader," in this section.

To subscribe to a newsgroup:

1. Click on the Add Newsgroups icon in the Newsgroups window.

A window that holds a hierarchical list of all the newsgroups appears. A hierarchy exists to organize the groups (for example, all groups beginning with alt are bunched together, all groups beginning with rec are together, and so forth).

2. Double-click on a hierarchy and then a subhierarchy (if subhierarchies are present) to see a list of the newsgroups.

> **3.** After finding a newsgroup of interest, select the group by clicking *once* on its name.
>
> **4.** Click on the Add button.

If you already know the exact name of a newsgroup of interest, just follow these steps:

> **1.** Click on the Expert Add icon found in the Newsgroups window.
>
> **2.** Type the newsgroup name.
>
> **3.** Click on the Add button.

Reading a subscribed newsgroup article

After you've subscribed to newsgroups of interest, you don't have to search out these groups each time you want to read an article in one or more of the groups. Instead, follow these steps to read an article:

> **1.** Click on the Read My Newsgroups icon found in the Newsgroups window.
>
> The Read My Newsgroups window appears.
>
> **2.** Double-click on the name of a newsgroup.
>
> A window holding a list of all threads in that newsgroup appears.
>
> **3.** Double-click on the name of a thread.
>
> A window with the first thread in it appears.
>
> **4.** To read the next article in the thread (if there is one), click on the Next Message button.

Replying to the author of an article

To send an e-mail message directly to the author of a displayed article (as opposed to posting a reply to the newsgroup for the world to see), follow these steps:

> **1.** Click on the Email to Author button.
>
> A Reply to Author window appears.
>
> **2.** Type your reply in the Response box.
>
> **3.** Click on the Send button.

Before being able to reply to an article, you must first subscribe to the newsgroup that the article appears in. After subscribing, click on the Read My Newsgroups button in the Newsgroups window to access the newsgroup articles.

See also "Subscribing to a newsgroup" and "Starting the AOL newsreader," in this section.

Posting a response to an article

To post a response to a displayed article (a response that is viewable by anyone who enters the newsgroup), follow these steps:

1. Click on the Reply to Group button.

A Reply window appears.

2. Type your reply in the Response box.

3. (*Optional*) Check the Copy Author of original message via Email check box if you'd also like to send a copy of your response directly to the author of the original article (a common courtesy to the author).

4. Click on the Send button.

You must be subscribed to a newsgroup before you can post a response to an article. After subscribing, access the newsgroup articles by clicking on the Read My Newsgroups button in the Newsgroups window.

See also "Subscribing to a newsgroup," in this section.

Posting an article for a new topic

If the newsgroup that you're in doesn't have an existing thread that answers your question or relates to your thoughts, start a new thread — a new series of articles on a single topic. From within the newsgroup list of threads, do the following:

1. Click on the Send New Message icon.

A Post New Message window appears.

2. Type an accurate, descriptive thread title in the Subject box.

3. Type the message in the Message field.

4. Click on the Send button.

You can only create a new thread in a newsgroup that you subscribe to. After subscribing, click on the Read My Newsgroups button in the Newsgroups window to access the newsgroup articles.

See also "Subscribing to a newsgroup" and "Starting the AOL newsreader," in this section.

Ignoring the threads in a newsgroup

After reading some of the threads in a newsgroup, you might want to mark all the remaining uninteresting threads as read. Then the next time you return to the same newsgroup, the articles in those threads won't reappear as new articles. To perform this task, click on the Mark All Read icon in the Newsgroups window.

See also "Starting the AOL newsreader," in this section.

Parental Control

AOL allows you to "black out" select newsgroups so that younger family members can't view their contents. From the Newsgroups window, click on the Parental Controls button. The window that appears provides the details of how to block certain newsgroups.

See also "Starting the AOL newsreader," in this section.

Unsubscribing to a newsgroup

1. Click on the Read My Newsgroups icon in the Newsgroups window.

   See also "Starting the AOL newsreader," in this section.

2. Select the group to unsubscribe to by clicking *once* on its name.

3. Click on the Remove button.

Exiting the AOL newsreader

After you've finished reading and posting newsgroup articles, click on the close box in the Newsgroups window to exit the newsreader.

See also "Starting the AOL newsreader," in this section.

CompuServe

CompuServe's MacCIM software uses the USENET Newsgroups window (shown in the next figure) as the "home base" for working with newsgroups. Read the section, "Starting the MacCIM newsreader," first. Follow the steps in that section to reach this important window.

Starting the MacCIM newsreader

1. Double-click on the Internet icon in the Browse window.

The Internet window appears.

2. Click on the Discussion Groups (Usenet) icon.

The Navigating window appears.

3. Double-click on the words USENET Newsreader (CIM).

Moving to a newsgroup

Before reading articles, you have to move to a particular newsgroup.

1. Double-click on the words Subscribe to Newsgroups in the USENET Newsgroups window.

A window that holds a hierarchical list of all the newsgroups appears. A hierarchy exists to organize the groups (for example, all groups beginning with alt are bunched together, all groups beginning with rec are together, and so forth).

2. Double-click on one of the hierarchies to see a list of the newsgroups in that hierarchy. To see more newsgroups, click on the Continued bar in the bottom of the window.

Subhierarchies may be within a hierarchy. If that's the case, continue double-clicking until you reach a list of newsgroups.

3. After you find a newsgroup of interest, click on the check box beside the newsgroup name.

4. Click on the Preview button.

A window holding a list of articles in that newsgroup appears.

Reading a newsgroup article

1. After moving to a newsgroup, click on a check box next to a thread (a topic) name within the newsgroup list of articles.

See also "Moving to a newsgroup," in this section.

2. Click on the Get button.

A window appears holding the text of the first message in the thread.

3. Read the first article in the thread.

4. If more articles are in the same thread, click on the > button found under the word *Article*.

To read an article in a group you're subscribed to, **see** the "Reading a subscribed newsgroup article" section.

Saving a newsgroup article

If you want to be able to refer back to an article of interest, choose File⇨Save while the article is in the front-most window. That saves the article as a text file.

Subscribing to a newsgroup

Instead of searching out and moving to one newsgroup each time you want to read that group's messages, find the group one time and then subscribe to it. CompuServe allows you to subscribe to any number of newsgroups.

All subscribed groups are easily accessible from the USENET Newsgroups window by double-clicking the words Access Your USENET Newsgroups. **See also** "Starting the MacCIM newsreader," in this section.

To subscribe to a newsgroup, follow these steps:

1. Double-click on the words Subscribe to Newsgroups in the USENET Newsgroups window.

A window that holds a hierarchical list of all the newsgroups appears. A hierarchy exists to organize the groups (for example, all groups beginning with alt are bunched together, all groups beginning with rec are together, and so forth).

2. Double-click on one of the hierarchies to see a list of the newsgroups in that hierarchy. To see more newsgroups, click on the Continued bar at the bottom of the window.

Subhierarchies may be within a hierarchy. If that's the case, continue double-clicking until you reach a list of newsgroups.

3. After finding a newsgroup of interest, click on the check box beside the newsgroup name.

4. Click on the Subscribe button.

If you already know the exact name of a newsgroup of interest, just follow these steps:

1. Double-click on the words Subscribe to Newsgroups in the USENET Newsgroups window.

   See also "Starting the MacCIM newsreader," in this section.

2. Click on the Subscribe By Name button in the Subscribe to Newsgroups window.

3. Type the name of the newsgroup.

4. Click on the OK button.

Reading a subscribed newsgroup article

After you've subscribed to some newsgroups of interest, you don't have to search out these groups each time that you want to read an article in one or more of the groups. Instead, follow these steps to read an article:

1. Double-click on the words Access Your USENET Newsgroups in the USENET Newsgroups window.

   The Access Newsgroups window appears.

2. Double-click on the name of a newsgroup.

   A window holding a list of all threads in that newsgroup appears.

3. Click the check box beside the name of a thread.

4. Click on the Get button.

   A window with the first thread in it appears.

5. To read the next article in the thread (if there is one), click on the right arrow (>) button.

Replying to the author of an article

To send an e-mail message directly to the author of a displayed article (as opposed to posting a reply to the newsgroup for the world to see), follow these steps:

1. Click on the Reply button.

   A Reply to USENET Message window appears.

2. Check the Send via E-mail check box (if it is not already checked).

3. Type your reply in the main box — the largest box in the window.

4. Click on the Send button.

Posting a response to an article

To post a response to a displayed article (a response that is viewable by anyone who enters the newsgroup), follow these steps:

1. Click on the Reply button.

A Reply to USENET Message window appears.

2. Check the Post to Newsgroup(s) check box (if it is not already checked).

3. (*Optional*) Check the Send via Email check box if you'd also like to send a copy of your response directly to the author of the original article (a common courtesy to the author).

4. Type your reply in the main box — the largest box in the window.

5. Click on the Send button.

Posting an article for a new topic

If the newsgroup that you're in doesn't have an existing thread that answers your question or relates to your thoughts, start a new thread — a new series of articles on a single topic. From within the newsgroup list of threads, do the following:

1. Click on the Create button.

A Create USENET Message appears.

2. Check the Post to Newsgroup(s) check box (if it is not already checked).

3. Type an accurate, descriptive thread title in the Subject box.

4. Type the message in the main box.

5. Click on the Send button.

Ignoring the threads in a newsgroup

After reading some of the threads in a newsgroup, you might want to mark all the remaining uninteresting threads as read. Then the next time you return to the same newsgroup, the articles in those threads won't reappear as new articles. To perform this task

1. Click on the check box beside each thread to ignore.

2. Then click on the Clear button.

Unsubscribing to a newsgroup

1. Double-click on the words "Access Your USENET Newsgroups" in the USENET Newsgroup window.

See also "Starting the MacCIM newsreader," in this section.

2. Select the group to unsubscribe to by clicking *once* on its name.

3. Click on the Remove button.

Exiting the MacCIM newsreader

When you've finished reading and posting newsgroup articles, exit the newsreader by clicking the Cancel button in each open newsreader window — including the Navigating window and the USENET Newsgroups window.

eWorld

eWorld uses its Internet Message Boards window (shown in the next figure) as the "home base" for working with newsgroups. Read the section, "Starting the eWorld newsreader," first. Follow the steps in that section to reach this important window.

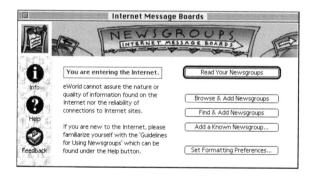

Starting the eWorld newsreader

1. Click on the Internet On-Ramp area of the introductory screen — referred to as the Town Square screen.

If this window isn't present, choose Places⇨Town Square from the menu bar.

The eWorld Internet window appears.

2. Click on the Newsgroups (Internet Message Boards) icon.

The Internet Message Boards window appears.

Moving to a newsgroup

Before reading articles, you must move to a particular newsgroup.

1. Click on the Browse & Add Newsgroups button in the Internet Message Boards window.

A window that holds a hierarchical list of all the newsgroups appears. A hierarchy exists to organize the groups (for example, all groups beginning with alt are bunched together, all groups beginning with rec are together, and so forth).

2. Double-click on one of the hierarchies to see a list of the newsgroups in that hierarchy. To see more newsgroups, click on the Continued bar at the bottom of the window.

You may find subhierarchies within a hierarchy. If that's the case, continue double-clicking until you find a list of newsgroups.

3. After finding a newsgroup of interest, double-click on the newsgroup name.

A window that holds a list of articles in that newsgroup appears.

Reading a newsgroup article

1. After moving to a newsgroup, double-click on a thread (a topic) name within the newsgroup list of articles.

See also "Moving to a newsgroup," in this section.

A window appears holding the text of the first message in the thread.

2. Read the first article in the thread.

3. If more articles are in the same thread, click on the Next arrow to read the next article.

To read an article in a group that you're subscribed to, see the "Reading a subscribed newsgroup article" section.

Saving a newsgroup article

If you want to be able to refer back to an article of interest, choose File⇨Save As while the article is in the front-most window. That saves the article as a text file.

Subscribing to a newsgroup

Instead of searching out and moving to one particular newsgroup each time that you want to read that group's messages, find the group one time and then subscribe to it. eWorld allows you to subscribe to any number of newsgroups.

All subscribed groups are then easily accessible from the Internet Message Boards window by clicking on the Read Your Newsgroups button. (*See also* "Starting the eWorld newsreader," in this section.)

To subscribe to a newsgroup, follow these steps:

1. Click on the Browse & Add Newsgroups button in the Internet Message Boards window.

   A window that holds a list of all the Usenet hierarchies appears.

2. Double-click on a hierarchy and then on a subhierarchy (if subhierarchies are present) to see a list of the newsgroups.

3. After finding a newsgroup of interest, select the group by clicking *once* on its name.

4. Click on the Add to Your Newsgroups button.

If you already know the exact name of a newsgroup of interest, just follow these steps:

1. Click on the Add a Known Newsgroup button found in the Internet Message Boards window.

2. Then type the newsgroup name.

3. Click on the Add button.

Reading a subscribed newsgroup article

After you've subscribed to some newsgroups of interest, you don't have to search out these groups each time you want to read an article in one or more of the groups. Instead, follow these steps to read an article:

1. Click on the Read Your Newsgroups button found in the Internet Message Boards window.

   The Your Newsgroups window appears.

2. Double-click on the name of a newsgroup.

   A window holding a list of all threads in that newsgroup appears.

3. Double-click on the name of a thread.

   A window with the first thread in it appears.

4. To read the next article in the thread (if there is one), click on the Next button.

Replying to the author of an article

To send an e-mail message directly to the author of a displayed article (as opposed to posting a reply to the newsgroup for the world to see), follow these steps:

1. Click on the Reply to Author button.

A Reply to Author window appears.

2. Type your reply in the main box — the largest box in the window.

3. Click on the Send Reply button.

Before you can reply to an article, you must first subscribe to the newsgroup that the article appears in. After subscribing, access the newsgroup articles by clicking on the Read Your Newsgroups button in the Internet Message Boards window.

See also "Subscribing to a newsgroup," in this section.

Posting a response to an article

To post a response to a displayed article (a response that is viewable by anyone who enters the newsgroup), follow these steps:

1. Click on the Reply button.

A Reply window appears.

2. Type your reply in the main box.

3. (*Optional*) Check the Mail a copy to the author of original message check box if you'd also like to send a copy of your response directly to the author of the original article (a common courtesy to the author).

4. Click on the Send Reply button.

You must be subscribed to a newsgroup before you can post a response to an article. After subscribing, access the newsgroup articles by clicking on the Read Your Newsgroups button in the Internet Message Boards window.

See also "Subscribing to a newsgroup," in this section.

Posting an article for a new topic

If the newsgroup that you're in doesn't have an existing thread that answers your question or relates to your thoughts, start a new thread — a new series of articles on a single topic. From within the newsgroup list of threads, do the following:

1. Click on the Create Thread button.

A Create Thread window appears.

2. Type an accurate, descriptive thread title in the Subject box.

3. Type the message in the main box.

4. Click on the Create button.

You can create a new thread only in a newsgroup that you subscribe to. After subscribing, access the newsgroup articles by clicking on the Read Your Newsgroups button in the Internet Message Boards window.

See also "Subscribing to a newsgroup," in this section.

Ignoring the threads in a newsgroup

After reading some of the threads in a newsgroup, you might want to mark all the remaining uninteresting threads as read. Then the next time you return to the same newsgroup, the articles in those threads won't reappear as new articles. To perform this task, click on the Mark All as Read button in the newsgroup's window.

Unsubscribing to a newsgroup

1. Click on the Read Your Newsgroups icon in the Internet Message Boards window.

See also "Starting the eWorld newsreader," in this section.

2. Select the group to unsubscribe to by clicking *once* on its name.

3. Click on the Remove Newsgroup button.

Exiting the eWorld newsreader

When you've finished reading and posting newsgroup articles, click on the close box of the Internet Message Boards window to exit the newsreader.

NewsWatcher

If you access the Internet through the use of a local Internet access provider, chances are good that the provider gave you a copy of the NewsWatcher software for working with newsgroups. The following figure shows the three main windows that NewsWatcher displays.

Starting the NewsWatcher newsreader

Double-click on the NewsWatcher icon in the desktop or, if you're
working from a palette of Internet utilities, on the NewsWatcher icon
in the palette.

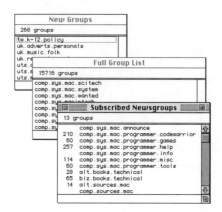

After NewsWatcher launches, three windows appear:

+ The *Subscribed Newsgroup* window lists the names of the
  newsgroups to which you are currently subscribed.

+ The *New Groups* window lists the names of new newsgroups —
  newsgroups that have come into existence since you last
  ran NewsWatcher.

+ The *Full Group List* window lists the thousands of newsgroups
  that NewsWatcher is aware of.

On rare occasions, the Full Group List window may not appear.
Should that happen, you can open the window by choosing
Windows⇨Full Group List.

Moving to a newsgroup

Before reading articles, you have to move to a particular newsgroup.

1. Scroll through the list of newsgroups until you find one
of interest.

2. Double-click on the name of a newsgroup.

A window that holds a list of newsgroup threads appears.

Reading a newsgroup article

1. After moving to a newsgroup, double-click on a thread (a topic) name within the newsgroup list of articles.

See also "Moving to a newsgroup," in this section.

A window that holds the text of the first message in the thread appears.

2. Read the first article in the thread.

3. If more articles are in the same thread, click on the down arrow icon found at the top right of the message to read the next article.

Saving a newsgroup article

If you want to be able to refer back to an article of interest, choose File⇨Save As while the article is in the front-most window. That saves the article as a text file.

Subscribing to a newsgroup

Instead of searching out and moving to one particular newsgroup each time that you want to read that group's messages, find the group one time and then subscribe to it. NewsWatcher allows you to subscribe to any number of newsgroups.

All subscribed groups are easily accessible from the Subscribed Newsgroups window. **See also** "Starting the NewsWatcher newsreader," in this section.

To subscribe to a newsgroup, follow these steps:

1. Scroll through the list of newsgroups until you find one of interest.

2. After finding a newsgroup of interest, select the group by clicking *once* on its name.

You can select more than one newsgroup to add by holding the Command key down while clicking once on each newsgroup name.

3. Choose Special⇨Subscribe.

4. Choose File⇨Save so that the added newsgroup appears in the Subscribed Newsgroups window each time that you run NewsWatcher.

Replying to the author of an article

To send an e-mail message directly to the author of a displayed article (as opposed to posting a reply to the newsgroup for the world to see), follow these steps:

1. Choose News⇨Reply.

A window holding the text of the message to which you're responding appears. This text appears so that the recipient of your e-mail has the context of his or her original message to which you are responding.

2. Type your reply in the main box — the largest box in the window.

3. If a check mark *doesn't* appear next to the Mail icon at the top of the window, click on that icon to check it.

Checking this icon tells NewsWatcher to e-mail your message to the author of the original post.

4. If a check mark *does* appear next to the News icon at the top of the window, click on that icon to uncheck it.

Unchecking this icon tells NewsWatcher to refrain from posting your message back to the newsgroup.

5. Click the Send button.

If you feel your correspondence with the author is important, you might want to document your mailings by keeping a copy of each message that you send to the author. To easily send yourself an e-mail copy of your message, place a check mark by the Self icon (the face icon that appears to the right of the Mail icon).

Posting a response to an article

To post a response to a displayed article (a response that is viewable by anyone who enters the newsgroup), follow these steps:

1. Choose News⇨Reply.

A window holding the text of the message to which you're responding appears. This text appears so that readers of the message that you're about to post have the context of the original message to which you are responding.

2. Type your reply in the main box — the largest box in the window.

3. If a check mark *doesn't* appear next to the News icon at the top of the window, click on that icon to check it.

Checking this icon tells NewsWatcher to post your message back to the newsgroup.

4. If you'd like to send the author of the original article an e-mail copy of your reply (a common courtesy to the author), make sure that a check mark *does* appear next to the Mail icon at the top of the window.

Posting an article for a new topic

If the newsgroup that you're in doesn't have an existing thread that answers your question or relates to your thoughts, start a new thread — a new series of articles on a single topic. From within the newsgroup list of threads, do the following:

1. Make sure that the newsgroup to which you want the new message to be posted is the front-most, or active, window.

2. Choose News⇨New Message.

   A new window appears.

3. Verify that the correct newsgroup is named after the Newsgroups label in the window.

   If the correct newsgroup is not named correctly, click the window's close box to close the window, and then click on the correct newsgroup window to bring it to the front. Then repeat steps 1 and 2.

4. Type an accurate, descriptive thread title in the Subject box.

5. Type the message in the main box — the largest box in the window.

6. Click on the Send button.

Ignoring the threads in a newsgroup

After reading some of the threads in a newsgroup, you might want to mark all the remaining uninteresting threads as read. Then the next time you return to the same newsgroup, the articles in those threads won't reappear as new articles. To perform this task

1. Choose Edit⇨Select All.

2. Then choose News⇨Mark Read.

   A check mark appears to the left of each thread title in the newsgroup window, indicating that each message is considered read.

Unsubscribing to a newsgroup

1. If the Subscribed Newsgroup window isn't the front window, bring it to the front by clicking on it.

2. Click once on the name of the newsgroup that you want to remove.

3. Choose Special⇨Unsubscribe.

4. Choose File⇨Save to save the change that you've just made.

Exiting the NewsWatcher newsreader

To exit the NewsWatcher newsreader, simply choose File⇨Quit.

Prodigy

Prodigy uses its Your USENET Newsgroup List window (shown in the next figure) as the "home base" for working with newsgroups. Read the section, "Starting the Prodigy newsreader," first. Follow the steps in that section to reach this important window.

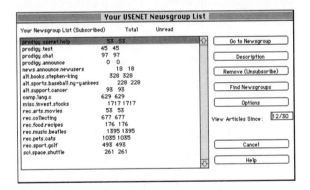

Starting the Prodigy newsreader

1. Choose Jump⇨Jump To.

2. Type **newsgroups** in the Jump box.

3. Click on the OK button.

The Internet USENET Newsgroups window appears.

4. If you *have* used newsgroups through Prodigy in the past, go to step 11 now. If you *haven't* used newsgroups in the past, you must first complete steps 5–10 to set newsgroup access control.

5. Click on the Newsgroups button.

6. In the window that opens, click on the Select Names button.

7. In the window that opens, click on your name.

8. Now click on the OK button.

9. In the window that opens, click on the Accept button.

10. Finally, in the window that opens, click on Go To USENET Newsgroups.

Now that Prodigy has given you newsgroup access, in the future you can skip steps 5–10.

11. Click on the Newsgroup button.

The Your USENET Newsgroup List window appears.

Moving to a newsgroup

Before reading articles, you have to move to a particular newsgroup:

1. Click on the Find Newsgroups icon in the Your USENET Newsgroup List window.

The Find a Newsgroup window appears.

2. Click on the All available Newsgroups radio button.

3. Click on the Find Now button.

4. Double-click on one of the hierarchies to see a list of the newsgroups in that hierarchy. To see more newsgroups, click on the Get More Newsgroups button.

You may find subhierarchies within a hierarchy. If that's the case, continue double-clicking until you reach a list of newsgroups.

5. After finding a newsgroup of interest, double-click on the newsgroup name.

A window holding a list of articles in that newsgroup appears.

Reading a newsgroup article

1. After moving to a newsgroup, double-click on a thread (a topic) name within the newsgroup list of articles.

See also "Moving to a newsgroup," in this section.

A window that holds the text of the first message in the thread appears.

2. Read the first article in the thread.

3. If more articles are in the same thread, click on the Next Article button to read the next article.

Saving a newsgroup article

If you want to be able to refer back to an article of interest, first display that article and then take the following steps:

1. Click on the Print/Save button.

2. In the window that opens, click on the Save As button to save the article as a text file.

Subscribing to a newsgroup

Instead of searching out and moving to one particular newsgroup each time that you want to read that group's messages, find the group one time and then subscribe to it. Prodigy allows you to subscribe to any number of newsgroups.

All subscribed groups are easily accessible from the Your USENET Newsgroup List window. *See also* "Starting the Prodigy newsreader," in this section.

To subscribe to a newsgroup, follow these steps:

1. Click on the Find Newsgroups icon in the Your USENET Newsgroup List window.

The Find a Newsgroup window appears.

2. Click on the All available Newsgroups radio button.

3. Click on the Find Now button.

4. Double-click on a hierarchy and then on a subhierarchy (if subhierarchies are present) to see a list of the newsgroups.

5. After finding a newsgroup of interest, select the group by clicking *once* on its name.

6. Click on the Add to Your Newsgroups button.

If you already know the exact name of a newsgroup of interest:

1. Click on the Find Newsgroups icon in the Your USENET Newsgroup List window.

2. Click on the Search Newsgroups for text pattern below radio button.

3. Then type the newsgroup name.

4. Click on the Find Now button.

The name of the one newsgroup appears.

5. Click on the Add to Your Newsgroups button to subscribe to it.

Replying to the author of an article

To send an e-mail message directly to the author of a displayed article (as opposed to posting a reply to the newsgroup for the world to see), follow these steps:

1. Click on the Respond button.

A Respond window appears.

2. Click on the Reply Privately to Author only button if it is not already selected.

3. Click on the OK button.

The Send A Private Reply window opens.

4. Type your reply in the main box — the largest box in the window.

5. Click on the Send button.

Posting a response to an article

To post a response to a displayed article (a response that is viewable by anyone who enters the newsgroup), follow these steps:

1. Click on the Respond button.

A Respond window appears.

2. Click on the Post Public Reply button if it is not already selected.

3. Click on the OK button.

A Post A Public Follow Up window opens.

4. Type your reply in the main box — the largest box in the window.

5. Click on the Post button.

Posting an article for a new topic

If the newsgroup that you're in doesn't have an existing thread that answers your question or relates to your thoughts, start a new thread — a new series of articles on a single topic. From within the newsgroup list of threads, do the following:

1. Click on the Post New Article button.

A Post A New Article window appears.

2. Type an accurate, descriptive thread title in the Subject box.

3. Type the message in the main box — the largest box in the window.

4. Click on the Post button.

Ignoring the threads in a newsgroup

After reading some of the threads in a newsgroup, you might want to mark all the remaining uninteresting threads as read. Then the next time you return to the same newsgroup, the articles in those threads won't reappear as new articles. To perform this task

1. Click on the Clear Articles button in the newsgroup's window.

2. In the Clear Articles window that opens, click on the Clear All Articles in Newsgroup radio button.

3. Then click on the OK button.

After clearing all the articles in a newsgroup, don't immediately attempt to return to that newsgroup. That is, don't double-click on the newsgroup's name from the Your USENET Newsgroup List window. This results in an error that causes you to be disconnected from Prodigy! You'll have to rerun the Prodigy software and reconnect.

Unsubscribing to a newsgroup

1. From the Your USENET Newsgroup List window, select the group to unsubscribe to by clicking *once* on its name.

See also "Starting the Prodigy newsreader," in this section.

2. Click on the Remove (Unsubscribe) button.

Exiting the Prodigy newsreader

When you've finished reading and posting newsgroup articles, click on the Cancel button in the Your USENET Newsgroup List window to exit the newsreader.

Proper Newsgroup Etiquette

Part III discusses e-mail etiquette — the important practice of being civil when sending e-mail. Everything covered in that part applies to posting newsgroup messages. Perhaps even more so.

An e-mail message is typically read by one person. A message posted to a newsgroup resides on a bulletin board accessible by anyone with Internet access. Your message has the potential to be read by millions of people. Keep that in mind when replying to some topic that upsets you! The following civilities are ones that you are strongly encouraged to abide by:

- ✦ **Don't *flame*.** Flaming is an outpouring of your frustration or outrage. Instead, hold your breath, count to ten, and then reply. If you disagree with a message, respond with counter points rather than simply ranting.

- ✦ **Avoid swearing or obnoxious language.**

- ✦ **Don't use all uppercase in a message.** RELEASE THE CAP LOCK KEY OR IT WILL LOOK LIKE YOU'RE YELLING!

- ✦ **Be careful when using sarcasm.** Unlike the face-to-face spoken word, which is accompanied by laughter, smiling, or a wink and a nod, the written word can be easlly misinterpreted. What you meant as humor may be perceived as nastiness. When you do use sarcasm, follow the sentence with a smiley :-) or a winking smiley ;-) to let the recipient know your intentions.

Part VI

File Downloading (FTP)

To move a file across the Internet, you "FTP it" from one Internet computer to another. *FTP,* or File Transfer Protocol, is a program that makes it possible for you to *download* (to copy a program from a remote computer to your Mac) programs from Internet FTP sites.

An *FTP site* (also called an FTP server, or FTP remote host) is a computer set up specifically to hold files. Many of the files on an FTP site are available for downloading by the public. That's you! And because any type of file — including software, graphics files, and text files — can be made available for FTP, you can amass a hard disk full of files for nothing more than the cost of the time that you're connected to the Internet.

In this part . . .

- ✓ Addresses of FTP sites
- ✓ Anonymous user ID and FTP site connections
- ✓ Passwords and FTP site connections
- ✓ Uncompressing downloaded files
- ✓ Connecting to an FTP site using AOL, CompuServe, eWorld, Fetch, and Prodigy
- ✓ Downloading a file using FTP from all of those same services

About Connecting to an FTP Site

To connect to an FTP site, you need to specify the site's address, your user ID, and a password.

+ **Address:** A site address typically begins with ftp. To tell your FTP software (the software that carries out the FTP file transfer, or download) that the address represents an FTP site, you precede the address with ftp:// as in ftp://ftp.apple.com.

This is generally true whether you're using the FTP software built into an online service (such as America Online) or separate FTP software supplied to you by a local Internet access provider (such as Fetch). If your FTP software *doesn't* recognize a site address that you know to be valid, try entering the address without the ftp:// part — your software may be automatically adding this part to the address that you enter.

+ **User ID:** If you have a personal account on the FTP site that you're connecting to (which is unlikely — unless you belong to the organization at which the site is located), then you have a username, or ID, that you should use. If you don't have an account (which is most likely), then type the word anonymous in place of a user ID.

+ **Password:** Again, if you have a personal account on a site, you've been issued a password. Otherwise, type in your Internet e-mail address in place of the password.

Some FTP software, such as the software built into most online services, includes a set of easy-to-access FTP sites — you just point-and-click to connect to one of them. For those sites, you don't need to enter the address, user ID, or password — your online service takes care of all of that!

Don't forget to check out Appendix B for a list of addresses and descriptions of many FTP sites that Mac users find of interest.

America Online

If you have an AOL account, you can easily FTP files to your Mac.

Connecting to an AOL-selected FTP site

If you don't know the addresses of any FTP sites, you can still connect to any one of several sites — AOL provides a list of several popular sites.

1. Choose Go To⇨Keyword.

The Keyword window appears.

2. Type **ftp**.

3. Click on the Go button.

The File Transfer Protocol window appears.

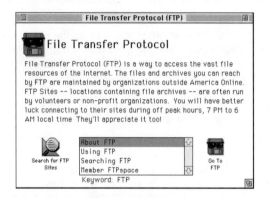

4. Click on the Go To FTP icon.

The Anonymous FTP window appears.

5. Double-click on the name of any site in the list to connect to that site.

Follow AOL's suggestion to connect during off-peak hours. Sites limit the number of people that can connect at any one time — so your best bet is to try to connect during late-night hours.

Connecting to a known FTP site

If you know the address of an FTP site that you'd like to visit, follow these steps to connect to it:

1. Choose Go To⇨Keyword.

The Keyword window appears.

2. Type **ftp**.

3. Click on the Go button.

The File Transfer Protocol window appears. *See also* "Connecting to an AOL-selected FTP site," in this section for a view of this window.

4. Click on the Go To FTP icon

The Anonymous FTP window appears. *See also* "Connecting to an AOL-selected FTP site," in this section for a view of this window.

5. Click on the Other Site button.

The Other Site window appears.

6. Type the address of the site to connect to.

7. Click on the Connect button.

Downloading a file

1. Connect to an FTP site.

See also "Connecting to an AOL-selected FTP site" or "Connecting to a known FTP site."

2. Double-click on folders until you reach a file of interest.

3. Click once on the name of the file that interests you.

4. Click on the Download Now icon.

A standard Save window opens.

5. Click on the Save button.

The File Transfer window appears. The progress of the download is shown in this window.

Disconnecting from an FTP site

To disconnect from a site, simply click on the close box of each window that lists folders or files at that site. The number of windows may vary, depending on how many folders you've double-clicked on in your search for a file to download.

CompuServe

If you have a CompuServe account, you have the capability to FTP files to your Mac.

Connecting to a CompuServe-selected FTP site

If you're new to FTP, you might not know the addresses of any FTP sites. CompuServe can help you in that regard — this service provides a list of some popular sites.

1. Double-click on the Internet icon in the Browse window.

The Internet window appears.

2. Click on the File Downloads (FTP) icon.

You might be faced with a window that lets you know that CompuServe is not responsible for the quality of files housed on FTP servers.

The File Transfer Protocol window appears.

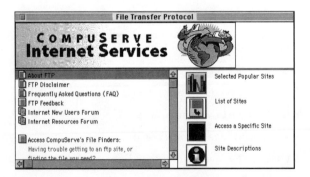

3. Click on the Selected Popular Sites icon.

The Selected Popular FTP Sites window appears.

4. Click on the icon of any site in the list to connect to that site.

The Access a Specific Site window appears.

5. Click on the OK button to connect to site.

Connecting to a known FTP site

If you know the address of an FTP site that you'd like to visit, follow these steps to connect to it:

1. Double-click on the Internet icon in the Browse window.

The Internet window appears.

2. Click on the File Downloads (FTP) icon.

The File Transfer Protocol window appears. ***See also*** "Connecting to a CompuServe-selected FTP site," in this section to view this window.

3. Click on the Access a Specific Site icon.

The Access a Specific Site window appears.

4. Type the address of the site to connect to.

5. Click on the OK button.

For the best chance of connecting to a site, make your attempt during off-peak hours. An FTP site allows a limited number of people to connect at any one time. Off-peak hours are considered to be early evening to early morning.

Downloading a file

1. Connect to an FTP site.

See also "Connecting to a CompuServe-selected FTP site" or "Connecting to a known FTP site," in this section.

2. Double-click on directory names in the Directories list on the left side of the Current Site window until you reach a directory that holds a file that interests you.

3. Click on in the check box that precedes the file name found in the Files list on the right side of the Current Site window.

4. Click on the Retrieve button.

A standard Save window opens.

5. Click on the Save button.

The File Transfer Status window appears. The progress of the download is shown in this window.

Disconnecting from an FTP site

To disconnect from a site, click on the Leave button in the Current Site window.

eWorld

As you see in this section, eWorld makes it easy to connect to an FTP server and download files.

Connecting to an eWorld-selected FTP site

If you're new to FTP, you might not know the addresses of any FTP sites. eWorld can help you in that regard — this service provides a list of some popular sites.

1. Click on the Internet On-Ramp area of the introductory window. (If the window isn't present, choose Places⇨Town Square.)

The eWorld Internet window appears.

2. Click on the Software Sources (Internet FTP Sites) icon.

The Internet Software Sources window appears.

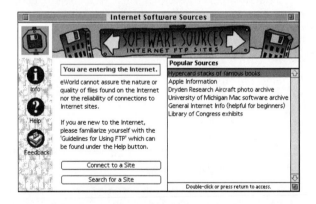

3. Double-click on the name of any site in the Popular Sources list to connect to that site.

Connecting to a known FTP site

If you know the address of an FTP site that you'd like to visit, follow these steps to connect to it:

1. Click on the Internet On-Ramp area of the introductory screen.

The eWorld Internet window appears.

2. Click on the Software Sources (Internet FTP Sites) icon.

The Internet Software Sources window appears. ***See also*** "Connecting to an eWorld-selected FTP site," in this section to view that window.

3. Click on the Connect to a Site button.

The Connect to a Site window appears.

4. Type the address of the site to connect to.

5. Click on the Connect button.

For the best chance of connecting to a site, make your attempt during off-peak hours. An FTP site allows a limited number of people to connect at any one time. Off-peak hours are considered to be early evening to early morning.

Downloading a file

1. Connect to an FTP site.

See also "Connecting to an eWorld-selected FTP site" or "Connecting to a known FTP site," in this section.

2. Double-click on folders until you reach a file of interest.

3. Click once on the name of the file of interest.

4. Click the Get It Now icon.

A standard Save window opens.

5. Click on the Save button.

The Get File window appears. The progress of the download is shown in this window.

Disconnecting from an FTP site

To disconnect from a site, simply click on the Close Connection button in the site window.

Fetch

If you connect to the Internet via a local access provider rather than a commercial online service, your provider may have included the popular Fetch program in its bundle of software. If so, follow the instructions in this section to download files to your Mac.

Starting the Fetch application

1. Double-click on the Fetch icon in the desktop or, if you're working from a palette of Internet utilities, on the Fetch icon in the palette.

When Fetch launches, an Open Connection window appears.

2. From this window, you can move to an FTP site. *See* the "Connecting to a Fetch-selected FTP site" section.

Your version of Fetch may prefill the Host box with the address of an FTP site.

```
╔═══════════ Open Connection... ═══════════╗
Enter host name, user name, and password
(or choose from the shortcut menu):

Host:        ftp.svcdudes.com

User ID:     anonymous

Password:    |

Directory:   /pub

Shortcuts:   ▼    ( Cancel )   [ OK ]
```

Connecting to a Fetch-selected FTP site

If you don't know the addresses of any FTP sites, you can still connect to any one of several sites — Fetch comes with the addresses of several popular sites built-in.

1. If the Open Connection window isn't already open, choose File⇨ Open Connection.

The Open Connection window appears.

2. With the cursor over the small down arrow button next to the Shortcuts label, click on and hold down the mouse button.

A pop-up menu listing some popular FTP sites is displayed. With the mouse button still held down, drag the cursor over a site name and release the mouse button.

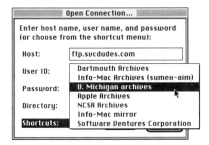

The address of the selected site appears in the box labeled Host.

3. Click on the OK button.

You'll have the best luck connecting to a site if you attempt to do so during evening hours. During the off-peak hours of about 7:00 p.m. to 7:00 a.m., there are less people attempting to connect to FTP sites — so your best bet is to try to connect during late-night hours.

Connecting to a known FTP site

If you know the address of an FTP site that you'd like to visit, follow these steps to connect to it:

1. If the Open Connection window isn't already open, choose File⇨Open Connection.

The Open Connection window appears.

2. Type the address of the site to connect to in the Host box.

3. Click on the OK button.

Downloading a file

1. Connect to an FTP site.

See also "Connecting to a Fetch-selected FTP site" or "Connecting to a known FTP site," in this section.

2. Double-click on folders until you reach a file that interests you.

3. Click on the name of the file to download.

4. Click on the Get File icon.

A standard Save window opens.

5. Click on the Save button.

The progress of the download is shown on the right side of the window.

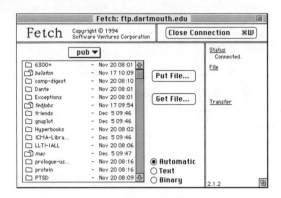

Disconnecting from an FTP site

To disconnect from a site, simply click on the Close Connection button.

Prodigy

Every major online service has a Mac version of a Web browser — except for Prodigy. In the Windows version of Prodigy, you use the Web browser to download files. In the Mac version, you will, too.

The following discussions are based on a prerelease Mac version of the Prodigy Web browser. By the time that you have a version of Prodigy that fully supports file downloading via FTP, things may work in a slightly different manner.

Connecting to an FTP site

Working with FTP on Prodigy differs from the approach used by other online services. Prodigy considers FTP an integrated part of the Web, so you access FTP via the Web. You can still use FTP with little knowledge of the Web. *See also* Part VIII of this book for more information about the World Wide Web.

A *URL* can be the address of a Web page. (*See also* Part VIII in this book.) It can also be the address of an FTP server. Type the FTP address, including the `ftp://` at the start of the address. Here's an example: `ftp://ftp.microsoft.com`.

If you know the address of an FTP site that you'd like to visit, follow these steps to connect to it:

1. Click on the small Web button at the bottom of the Prodigy window.

The World Wide Web window appears.

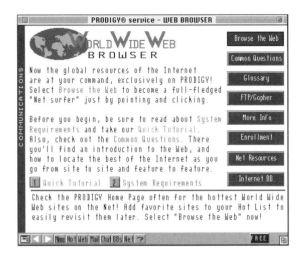

2. Click on the Browse the Web button.

The Web Browser window appears. The following figure shows what you'll see if your version of Prodigy *doesn't* yet support the Web browser.

3. Type the address of the site to connect to in the Document URL box.

4. Click on the Go To button.

For the best chance of connecting to a site, make your attempt during off-peak hours. An FTP site allows a limited number of people to connect at any one time. Off-peak hours are considered to be early evening to early morning.

Downloading a file

1. Use the Web browser to connect to an FTP site.

  See also "Connecting to an FTP site," in this section.

  A window holding a list of folders (directories) and files appears.

2. Click on folder names until you reach a file of interest.

3. Click on the name of a file to start downloading that file.

Disconnecting from an FTP site

To disconnect from a site, simply click on the close box of each window that lists folders or files at that site.

Uncompressing Downloaded Files

Files that are stored on an Internet FTP site are often stored in a compressed format. Before placing a file at a site, the file *uploader* (the person who placed the file on the FTP server in the first place) uses special software to *compress,* or shrink, the file. Since the file is smaller, you can download it quickly — saving you time and money.

If you download a file that's been compressed, you need to uncompress it to return it to its original size and make it usable. A variety of utility programs are designed to do just that one task — to uncompress files. In the Mac community, the most popular are:

✦ Aladdin Systems' StuffIt Expander

✦ Bill Goodman's Compact Pro

You can tell if a file is compressed and what compression utility program was used to compress it, by examining the file's *extension* — the part of the file name that follows the dot. For example, a file named Juggernaut.sit was compressed with the StuffIt program (sit) and, therefore, needs to be uncompressed with StuffIt Expander.

The following is a brief summary of the most common file extensions you'll find on Macintosh files that have been compressed.

.cpt

A file with the extension .cpt was compressed using Compact Pro. To uncompress such a file you may or may not need to own a copy of Compact Pro. Compact Pro allows you to compress a file in one of two ways.

One method requires that a person own a copy of Compact Pro in order to uncompress the file; the other doesn't.

This second method, the method that generates a *self-extracting* file, is of course the preferred method. A file that's been compressed in a self-extracting format should have a .sea (for self-extracting archive) extension, but it might have been given a .cpt extension instead. In either case, just double-click on the file's icon to uncompress the file. If it doesn't uncompress, you need a copy of Compact Pro.

.hqx

This extension indicates that the file is in Macintosh Binhex format. The compression utility program named Binhex 5.0 can be used to uncompress this type of file. StuffIt Expander also does the trick.

.sea

A file with the .sea extension is a self-extracting archive file — one that can be uncompressed without the aid of a file compression utility program. Just double-click on the file's icon. ***See also*** ".cpt," in this section for more information.

.sit

The .sit extension means that the file was compressed using StuffIt. StuffIt is a commercial program that you must pay for. However, a trimmed-down version of StuffIt is available for free. The StuffIt Expander program can't stuff, or compress, files. But it can unstuff, or uncompress them.

Utility programs, such as StuffIt Expander, Compact Pro, and Binhex, can be found in the file libraries of online services, such as America Online and CompuServe — available for just the few minutes it takes to download.

Part VII

Searching for Files

Part VI showed you how to download a file from an FTP server. Before you can do that, however, you must first *find* the file of interest. Considering that the thousands of FTP sites, which are part of the Internet, make up an interconnection of unrelated computers holding millions of files, finding a file sounds like a daunting task.

Internet *file-searching utilities (or resources),* such as Archie, Gopher, and WAIS, speed up this search by maintaining lists of files. Rather than traverse to every FTP site during a search, these search resources check their lists for a file that matches your search description. As an added bonus, some of these search resources also allow you to FTP, or download, a file as well.

In this part . . .

- ✔ A description of the various Internet file searching resources, or utilities: Archie, Gopher, Veronica, and WAIS

- ✔ When to use which resource

- ✔ Using Archie to file-search FTP servers

- ✔ Using Gopher and Veronica to information-seek in Gopherspace

- ✔ Using WAIS to search text databases

- ✔ File-searching from the online services: AOL, CompuServe, eWorld, and Prodigy

- ✔ File-searching from resources, such as Anarchie and TurboGopher, that are used with local access providers

- ✔ Downloading a file from online services and from local access providers

About Searching Resources

You can use a variety of resources to search for files on the Internet. As you read the description of each, be aware that your Internet access service most likely supports one or more of these utilities — but it's unlikely that you'll have all of the utilities at your disposal. Check out the section in this part that is specific to the service that you use.

Archie

To find and retrieve a file on the Internet, you can start by using the searching resource, Archie. To use Archie, basically you

1. Provide an Archie client with the address of an Archie server and a word (or words) that makes up part or all of the file name that you are interested in.

 The Archie client searches the Archie servers and returns a list of matching file names.

2. Use your Archie client to download one of the matched files to your Mac.

An *Archie client* is a program that you use to connect to an Archie server. An *Archie server* holds lists of FTP sites. ***See also*** Appendix B for a list of some Archie server addresses that you can use for performing file searches with Archie.

See also "Searching with Archie" and "Downloading a file," later in this part for more detailed information.

Gopher

Gopher is a resource used to *browse* information on the Internet instead of actually searching for a file. Consider Gopher one big Internet menu system. Organizations and — on occasion — individuals from around the world have established their own Gopher servers.

Each Gopher is a menu of items. For example, an item might be

 ✦ A file

 ✦ Another menu that takes you a layer deeper into the Gopher — like folders within folders

Most interesting of all, an item might lead, or point, to a different Gopher server altogether. This linking of Gophers throughout the world is called *Gopherspace*, and it's what makes the concept of the

Gopher so powerful. Once you finally find a file of interest, there's no telling where you traveled on the Internet to reach that file.

Be aware that Gopher won't turn up everything that's on the Internet. Someone has to *index,* or add, an item in order for it to appear in a Gopher search.

Gopher servers are notorious for being "flakey" — connections often fail. If you can't connect to a Gopher, select a different Gopher site and try the search again.

See also Appendix A for a list of some Gopher server addresses that you can use to start your searching.

Veronica

Veronica is a Gopher-searching resource that you can use to search for specific files. Where you use Gopher to meander about the Internet poking around for something interesting, you use Veronica to search for something more specific.

When you tell Veronica to search for files that include a specific word or words, Veronica searches all the Gophers for you. Then Veronica compiles a list of the results. This list of the results becomes a Gopher. For example, clicking on an item in the list takes you to that file.

WAIS

WAIS (pronounced *ways*) stands for Wide Area Information Service. WAIS is a text-searching resource that searches through several hundred sets (or sources, or databases) of information. Each information source holds one topic (such as presidential speeches). WAIS is very efficient, but it has one large limitation: If a WAIS source doesn't exist for the topic that interests you, you're out of luck—at least as far as a WAIS search goes. You can still try one of the other search methods, such as Gopher.

Which search method should you use?

The search method that you use depends on two factors:

+ What your service provider allows

+ What you're searching for

Different online services offer different search tools — some services offer more than others.

If you access the Internet through a local access provider, you have more options — you don't have to rely on what the online services provide. Instead, you can use powerful search software such as TurboGopher (*see also* "TurboGopher," later in this part).

Given the choice of search methods, consider these points:

+ If you know the name of the file that you're searching for, consider using Archie.

+ If you're researching a topic and you're looking for text files concerning a general topic, consider browsing the Internet using Gopher.

+ If you're doing a Gopher search for a text file and you have an idea of a word or words that are in the name of files that interest you, perform a Veronica search.

+ If you haven't found enough information using Gopher, try a WAIS search to find material that hasn't been indexed for Gopher.

Finally, if you have an account with one of the major online services such as AOL or CompuServe, consider skipping the Internet altogether! Before venturing out into the unknown of the Net, try looking in one of the software libraries maintained on your own online service.

America Online

America Online's Gopher service differs from most in that it is actually a combination of Gopher and WAIS search resources. The details of exactly what resource is used in any one search is kept hidden from you. Instead, you just click on folders that you want, and AOL decides what to do next.

If you plan on accessing the World Wide Web from America Online, then you'll be pleased to find out that the AOL Web Browser has a Gopher menu option that also allows you to make Gopher searches. ***See also*** Part VIII of this book for details.

Starting Gopher

1. Choose Go To⇨Keyword.

The Keyword window appears.

2. Type **gopher**.

3. Click on the Go button.

The Gopher & WAIS window appears.

Searching with Gopher

You can use AOL's Gopher searching to browse through folders to find files that are of interest.

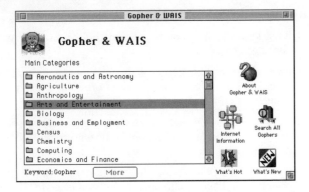

1. In the Gopher & WAIS window, double-click on a folder that interests you.

2. Continue clicking on folders until you find a file that interests you.

3. Double-click on the file that interests you.

A window that holds the file's text contents appears.

4. To save the contents of the file, choose File⇨Save As.

The following figure shows a Mac screen after a typical Gopher search. I double-clicked on several folders to open a text file about volcanoes.

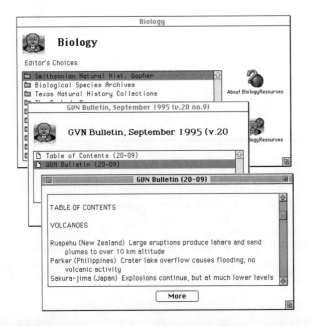

Searching with Veronica

To quickly search a variety of Gophers for a specific topic, perform a Veronica search:

1. Click on the Search All Gophers icon in the Gopher & WAIS window.

See also "Starting Gopher," in this section.

The Search all Gophers with Veronica window appears.

2. Type one or more words describing the topic that you're searching for.

3. Click on the Search button.

The folder and file names resulting from the search appear in the window.

4. To view the file's text contents, double-click on the file.

5. To save a text file, simply choose File⇨Save As.

Anarchie

Anarchie (pronounced *anarchy* rather than *an archie*) is an Archie search utility and FTP resource rolled into a single program. Anarchie is also one of the most powerful Internet search resources available to Mac users. Unfortunately, you can only use it if you have an account through a local access provider. Online services such as AOL and eWorld don't support Anarchie.

Your local access provider supplied you with Internet resource software — but Anarchie might not be a part of that package. Don't despair — Anarchie is a $10 shareware program that can be downloaded from the software libraries of online services or downloaded from any number of FTP archives.

See also Appendix B for a listing of a few FTP sites that are sure to carry this program.

Preparing to start Anarchie

When Anarchie (remember, it's pronounced *anarchy*) is launched, it loads information from a system extension (a "behind-the-scenes" piece of software stored in the Extensions folder of your System Folder) named *Internet Config* and a preferences file. If you have the Anarchie program but haven't yet used it, you need to do some easy — but very important — preliminary set-up chores.

You need to follow these steps the *first* time that you use Anarchie —
not *each* time you use Anarchie:

1. Double-click on the Internet Config icon in the desktop.

Because the Internet Config program accompanied Anarchie, you
should find it near your Anarchie program. The *Internet Config
program* is an installer program that will add a file to your System
Folder.

If you have the Internet Config system extension in your System
Folder, the Internet Preferences window appears, and you can
skip to step 4.

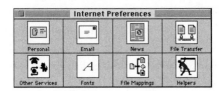

If you don't have the Internet Config system extension in your
System Folder (and you probably don't), an alert window
appears with a message telling you that the Internet Config
Extension is not installed. Go on to step 2.

2. Click on the Install button.

An alert window with a message telling you that installation was
successful appears.

3. Click on the OK button.

The Internet Preferences window appears.

4. Click on the Email icon in the Internet Preferences window.

The Email window appears.

5. Type your e-mail address (as used with your local Internet
access account) in the Email Address box.

Email	
Email Address:	dsydow@interramp.com
Mail Account:	
Mail Password:	
SMTP Host:	
Mail Headers:	

6. Click on the Internet Preferences window to bring it to the front of the screen.

7. Click on the File Transfer icon in the Internet Preferences window.

The File Transfer window appears.

8. Click on the box to the right of the Archie Server and select an Archie server name from the pop-up menu.

Remember: To select from the pop-up menu, continue to depress the mouse button while dragging the cursor to an Archie server name. Release the mouse to make the selection.

9. Repeat step 7 for the Info-Mac Server and the UMich Server in the File Transfer window.

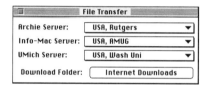

10. Click on the Internet Downloads button.

A standard Select folder window appears.

11. Use the pop-up menu at the top of the window and/or click on folder names in the window's list to move to the folder in which you want Anarchie to store downloaded files.

12. Click on the Select button when it displays the name of the desired folder.

13. Choose File⇨Save.

14. Choose File⇨Quit.

Starting Anarchie

1. Before running Anarchie, use your Internet access software to connect to the Internet.

2. Once connected, double-click on the Anarchie icon on the desktop.

The Bookmarks window opens. This window lists numerous Internet FTP servers. You can double-click on any one of them to connect to it.

Searching with Archie

1. Choose File⇨Archie.

The Archie window appears.

The Server box holds the name of the Archie server that you selected when you ran Internet Config (*see also* "Before starting Anarchie," in this section).

2. (Optional) To select a different Archie server, click on the down arrow icon to the right of the Server box and choose a server from the pop-up menu of Archie servers.

3. Type all or part of the name of the file to search for in the Find box. If you don't know the exact name of the file, try entering several characters that you think may be a part of the complete file name.

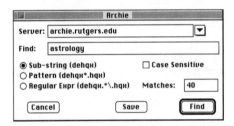

4. Click on the Find button.

Anarchie performs an Archie search of FTP sites. The results of the search — files names that contain your search string — are displayed in the window that appears.

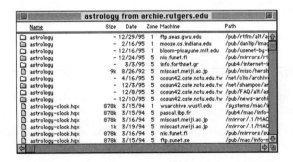

Downloading a file

The Anarchie program can do more than just search for files. Once you find a file, Anarchie can FTP it to your hard drive.

1. Perform an Archie search.

See also "Searching with Archie," in this section.

A window showing the search results appears.

2. Double-click on the name of the file to download.

Anarchie automatically connects to the FTP server that holds the file and then FTPs the file.

For each file in the search results window, Anarchie lists the address of the FTP server and the *path* (the folder hierarchy at the server) that leads to the file. If you simply double-click on the file to download it, this information isn't needed. If, however, you're interested in finding out what else is at a particular site, this information is invaluable: You can use the FTP address with your FTP utility (whether you have a utility built into your online service or you have a separate program like Fetch) to connect to this FTP site and browse through the server. *See also* Part VI for more information on FTP and Fetch.

CompuServe

As of this writing, CompuServe doesn't provide members with any of the powerful Internet file-searching resources found on other online services.

To make up for a lack of Internet search utilities, CompuServe offers these few recommendations to its members:

+ **Ask other users:** Experienced CompuServe members may know just where to go to find a particular file.

+ **Read the Index Files:** Many FTP servers maintain index files listing the names of all the files that they provide. Look in the server's top level directory or in the pub directory. This type of file usually includes index in its name. Otherwise, the file name is ls-lR, followed by an extension. An ls-lR index file is usually compressed, so you need to download it, uncompress it, use a word processor to read it offline, and then download the file of interest.

+ **Read the** README **file:** Some FTP servers have a README file that holds important information about that server. Such files sometimes contain information on where to find files of interest.

eWorld

eWorld has limited support for searching for Internet files. Instead of working directly with a search resource such as Gopher, you rely on the Search for a Site button in the Internet Software Sources window — as you see in the next figure.

If you plan on accessing the World Wide Web from eWorld, then you'll be pleased to know that the eWorld Web Browser has a Gopher menu item that allows you to perform true Gopher searches. *See also* Part VIII in this book for information on the Web and this Gopher utility.

Entering the eWorld FTP area

1. Click on the Internet On-Ramp area of the introductory screen.

The eWorld Internet window appears.

2. Click on the Software Sources (Internet FTP Sites) icon.

The Internet Software Sources window appears.

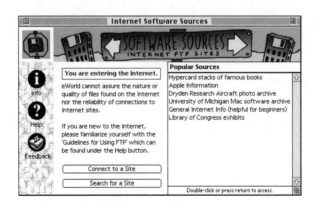

Searching for Internet files

1. Enter the eWorld FTP area.

See also "Entering the eWorld FTP area," in this section.

2. Click on the Search for a Site button.

The Find window appears.

3. Type a word or words that describe your interest.

4. Click on the Find button.

The results of the search are listed in the main box of the Find window.

5. Double-click on a site address to get information about that site.

A window with site and file information appears.

6. Select the site address using the mouse and then copy it by choosing Edit⇨Copy.

7. Click on the Internet Software Sources window to bring it to the front.

8. Click on the Search for a Site button in the Internet Software Sources window.

The Other Site window appears.

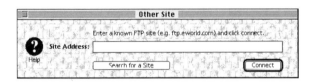

9. Paste the site address into the Site Address box by choosing Edit⇨Paste.

10. Click on the Connect button.

eWorld connects you to the FTP site.

11. Double-click on folders within the site to find a file of interest.

The following figure shows a Mac screen after a typical eWorld Internet file-search.

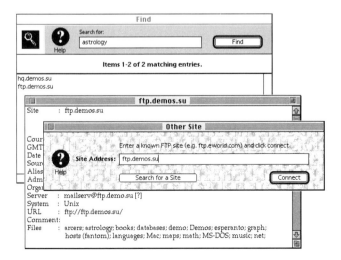

When I search for the topic of astrology, two FTP sites appear. Double-clicking on one site displays information about that site. The address of that site is then automatically added to the Other Site window so that eWorld can connect to it.

Prodigy

Every major online service has a Mac version of a Web browser — except for Prodigy. In the Windows version of Prodigy, you use the Web browser to perform a Gopher search. The Mac version will use this approach as well. The following discussions are based on a pre-release Mac version of the Prodigy Web browser. By the time you have a version of Prodigy that fully supports Gopher searches, things may work in a slightly different manner.

The Prodigy Gopher resource is an integrated part of the Prodigy World Wide Web Browser. You can still perform a Gopher search with little knowledge of the Web. *See also* Part VIII of this book for more information on the World Wide Web.

A *URL* can be the address of a Web page. (*See also* Part VIII of this book.) It can also be the address of a Gopher server. Be sure to include `gopher://` at the beginning of the address. Here's an example: `gopher://gopher.micro.umn.edu`. If you know the address of a gopher server (and now you *do* know at least one), you can perform a Gopher search.

Follow these steps to connect to a Gopher server:

1. Click on the small Web button at the bottom of the Prodigy window.

The World Wide Web window appears.

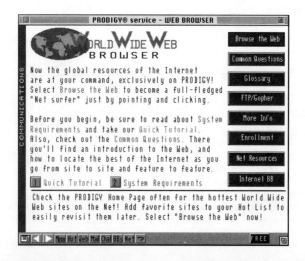

2. Click on the Browse the Web button.

The Web Browser window appears.

The following figure shows what you'll see if you *don't* have a version of Prodigy that includes a Web browser.

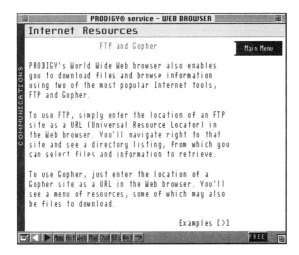

3. Type the address of the Gopher server to connect to in the Document URL box located near the top of the browser.

4. Click on the Go To button located to the right of the URL box.

TurboGopher

If you connect to the Internet from a local access provider rather than a commercial online service, your provider may have included the TurboGopher program in its bundle of software. If so, follow the instructions in this section to search for files and download them to your Mac.

Starting TurboGopher

To launch TurboGopher

1. Connect to the Internet using your Internet access software.

2. Double-click on the TurboGopher icon in the Finder.

If you're working from a palette of Internet utilities, connect to the Internet and then double-click on the TurboGopher icon in the palette.

When TurboGopher launches, you are automatically connected to the University of Minnesota Gopher server. From this Home Gopher window, you can perform Gopher searches.

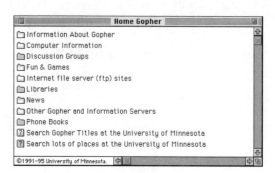

Searching with Gopher

1. Double-click on an interesting folder in the Home Gopher.

2. Continue clicking on folders until you find a file that interests you.

3. Double-click on the file.

If the file is a text file, a window that holds the text contents of the file appears. If the file is a program, TurboGopher automatically downloads the file for you.

4. If the file is a text file, you can save its contents by choosing File⇨Save As.

Searching with Veronica

To quickly search a variety of Gophers for a specific topic, perform a Veronica search.

1. Double-click on the Other Gopher and Information Servers folder in the Home Gopher window.

The Other Gopher and Information Servers window appears.

2. Double-click on the Search titles in GopherSpace using veronica folder in the Other Gopher and Information Servers window.

The Search titles in GopherSpace using veronica window appears.

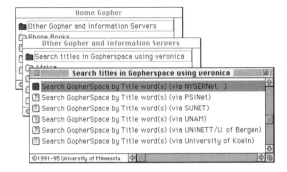

3. Double-click on one of the Search GopherSpace question mark icons in the Search titles in Gopherspace using veronica window.

A Find what? window appears.

4. Type a word or words to search for.

5. Click on the Find button.

TurboGopher searches for file's with names that include your search string. After the search is complete, a window displaying the results appears.

6. Double-click on the file of interest.

If the file is a text file, a window that holds the file's text contents appears. If the file is a program, TurboGopher automatically downloads the file for you. Before doing so, a Save window opens in which you should type a name for the file.

7. If the file is a text file, you can save its contents by choosing File⇨Save As.

Part VIII

The World Wide Web

While many people may talk about the Web as if it were something *different* than the Internet, it is actually another *part* of the Internet. Not just a bit part, though. Consider the Web the future of the Internet.

In this part . . .

- ✔ Graphics and the Web
- ✔ Understanding Uniform Resource Locators (URLs)
- ✔ Navigating the Web
- ✔ Using America Online to browse the Web
- ✔ Using CompuServe to browse the Web
- ✔ Using eWorld to browse the Web
- ✔ Using Netscape Navigator to browse the Web
- ✔ Using Prodigy to browse the Web

About Web Basics

The World Wide Web is another part of the Internet — and what a part it is! Most people consider the Web to be the future of the Internet.

Graphics and the Web

Much of the Internet is *text-based*. That is, information comes to you in the form of words and numbers rather than pictures. For many tasks, like the ones listed here, text-based information is just fine.

- ✦ **E-mail:** Like a phone call to someone, written words to a person are usually sufficient — you don't need graphics to say "Hello" or to ask a question.

- ✦ **Newsgroups:** Words generally suffice for the primary use of a newsgroup: making inquiries and exchanging ideas.

- ✦ **Mailing lists:** Like newsgroups, mailing lists are used for the exchange of information.

- ✦ **FTP:** A file stored on an Internet FTP server may contain graphics that you see after you download it, but those graphics don't need to be displayed while the file's on the Net.

When do you want to see graphics on the Internet? Here are a few cases where graphics are helpful:

- ✦ **Advertising:** A business that's selling a product on the Internet can better sell that product if people can see it before they buy it.

- ✦ **Promotion:** A business that is trying to sell *itself* — to promote itself — can capture people's attention by displaying a fancy company logo.

- ✦ **Task Facilitation:** Graphics can simplify some tasks; clicking on an icon or a picture is often more intuitive than selecting from a text menu.

The World Wide Web is a part of the Internet that addresses the three preceding points. Unlike the rest of the Internet, a Web page, or screen of information, usually uses graphics.

Uniform Resource Locators (URLs)

Like everything else on the Internet, to get to a Web page, you need to know its address. Web page addresses have a special name — *URLs,* or Uniform Resource Locators. A URL isn't something that you usually memorize — it's a long, awkward-looking string of letters and a few symbols. Here's a typical URL:

```
http://www.metrowerks.com/products/books/specials.html
```

A URL consists of three parts:

◆ The document (page) type followed by a colon and two slashes (`http://`). For a Web page, the document type is always `http` — that stands for hypertext.

◆ The host name of the computer on which the page resides. In the preceding example, the host computer is `www.metrowerks.com`.

◆ The path name to the file on the host computer that contains the information that is displayed as a page. The path to the file that holds the Web page information in the example is `/products/books/specials.html`. In that example, the information that will be displayed can be found in a `specials.html` file in the `books` folder that, in turn, is in the `products` folder. While the path to the file isn't important to you, the path is important to the Web browser — the browser needs to know how to access the file on the host computer.

TIP

Sometimes you encounter an address that doesn't have a path name, such as `http://www.metrowerks.com`. An address without a path name takes you to a main page from which you may be able to navigate to other pages associated with that main page.

In this example, moving to `http://www.metrowerks.com` takes you to the main page of a Macintosh programming company named Metrowerks. On that page, you find several hypertext links. Each link leads to a Metrowerks Web page that has its own URL. For instance, one of these links leads you to the Web page with the URL `http://www.metrowerks.com/products/index.html` — the Metrowerks Web page that lists the products that this company sells.

WARNING!

When you type a URL into your Web browser, type carefully.

◆ The Web browser understands only a URL that is correct — not one that is close to being correct.

◆ Make sure that you type the URL as it is written — use the same case (the same use of capitalization).

TIP

Documents other than Web pages can have URLs. For instance, you can travel to an FTP document by prefixing the FTP address with `ftp://`, as in `ftp://ftp.amug.org`. The same concept applies to a Gopher site — you can use the Gopher server address prefixed with `gopher://`, as in `gopher://gopher.usc.edu`.

Navigating the Web

To start your travels on the Web, you need to know the address, or URL, of at least one Web page. *See also* "Uniform Resource Locators (URLs)" in this section for additional information and Appendix C for a list of Web page addresses. Fortunately, you can travel about quite a bit without knowing the URL of every page that you visit — thanks to hypertext links.

When you click on a *hypertext link* on a Web page, you are automatically taken to a different Web page. A hypertext link can appear in any of several forms:

✦ A word, or words, that appear in a color different from the rest of the text on the page

✦ A word, or words, that are underlined

✦ An icon

✦ A picture (usually framed)

The beauty of a hypertext link is that it eliminates the need to know the URL of the page that you're about to be transported to — the designer of the Web page that you're currently on handled that detail.

America Online

The AOL Web browser offers America Online members an easy, intuitive way to browse the World Wide Web.

Obtaining the AOL Web browser

America Online doesn't have a built-in Web browser — AOL uses a separate software program. When you obtained your AOL software, it might not have come with this Web browser program. AOL provides this software to AOL users free of charge — you just need to download it from America Online.

If you don't have an Online Browser folder in the America Online folder on your hard drive, follow these steps to get a copy:

1. Choose Go To⇨Keyword.

The Keyword window appears.

2. Type **upgrade**.

3. Click on the Go button.

The AOL for Macintosh window appears.

4. Click on the Download Now icon.

The Please Note window appears.

5. Click on the Continue button.

The Mac Upgrade Software Library window appears.

6. Double-click on AOL Browser Only (2 of 2) in the list of files.

A window describing the AOL Web browser appears.

7. Copy or print the install instructions that appear in the window.

8. Click on the Download Now button.

AOL downloads the Web browser to your hard drive.

Starting the AOL Web browser

Before you can navigate the Web from your America Online account, you need to start the AOL Web browser.

1. Connect to AOL if you haven't already done so.

2. Choose Go To⇨Keyword.

The Keyword window appears.

3. Type **web**.

4. Click on the Go button.

The small World Wide Web window appears.

5. Click on the World Wide Web icon in the World Wide Web window.

If an alert window with a message saying that you must be connected to America Online appears, ignore it by clicking on the OK button. Wait a minute or more while AOL connects to the Web and loads the AOL home page.

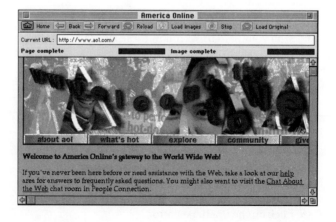

Changing the home page

Each time that you start the AOL Web browser, you find yourself at
AOL's own home page. You can use the home page as your starting
point for navigating the Web, or you can choose any other Web page
to be your home page.

1. Choose Edit⇨Configure.

The AOL Internet Configuration window appears.

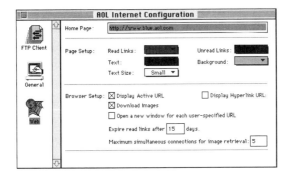

2. Click on the Web icon.

3. Type the URL of the Web page that you want to use as the new
home page.

The next time that you connect to the Web, and each time
thereafter, the page you entered will be the one at which AOL
starts.

4. Click on the window's close box to close the window.

Following a hypertext link

Hypertext links appear as colored words (or as underlined words)
within the rest of a page's text. Icons or pictures that are usually
framed may also be links.

1. Click on a hypertext word, icon, or picture to follow that link.

The AOL browser traverses the Web to find and then load the
document (page) that the link points to. The Opening connection label near the top of the browser window changes to a Page
label. The progress bar to the right of the label indicates the
loading progress of the page.

2. Click on the Stop icon if the loading takes too long; otherwise, wait for the page to load.

3. To return to the page that you came from, click on the Back arrow icon.

Turning image-loading off

Images that appear on pages (such as pictures and icons) are optional — they add to the Web experience, but they aren't neces-sary — for viewing the text of a page. If the loading of pages takes too long (usually because your modem is slower than 28.8K), you can set the browser so that it won't load images.

See also Part II for additional information on modem speeds.

1. Choose Edit⇨Configure.

The AOL Internet Configuration window appears.

2. Click on the Web icon.

3. Uncheck the Download Images check box.

4. Click on the window's close box to close the window.

5. If the Always Load Images item in the Web menu *is* checked, choose it now to uncheck it.

Web pages that you visit will display a simple, generic icon in place of graphic images. A page that you've already visited during the current session, however, still displays images if you return to that page. The AOL browser retains this image information and reloads the image quicker than it loads an image it encounters for the first time.

Turning image-loading on

If you've turned off image-loading and now want to turn image-loading back on, follow these steps:

1. Choose Edit⇨Configure.

The AOL Internet Configuration window appears.

2. Click on the Web icon.

3. Check the Download Images check box.

4. Click on the window's close box to close the window.

5. If the Always Load Images item in the Web menu *isn't* checked, choose it now to check it.

Moving to a URL

You can click on the Back arrow icon and Forward arrow icon to move to the Web pages that you've just visited. To move to a completely different Web page, follow these steps:

1. Choose Services⇨Open URL.

The Uniform Resource Locator window appears.

2. Type the URL that you wish to move to.

See also the "Uniform Resource Locators (URLs)" section near the beginning of this part for more information on the format of a URL.

Here is an even faster way:

1. Highlight the text in the Current URL field of the browser window.

2. Type the URL in this field.

You can also use copy and paste to copy the URL from another window and paste it into the Current URL field.

3. Once you've entered the URL, press the Return key to tell the browser to find and load the page.

4. Click on the OK button.

The AOL browser finds and loads the desired page.

Saving a URL in your hot list

If you reach a page that you are interested in and feel that you want to return to that page during another Web session, save the page's URL in your hot list. The *hot list* is the term AOL uses for an editable list of URLs. (Other Web browsers refer to saved URLs as bookmarks.)

1. With the page displayed in the browser, choose Services⇨Add To Main Hot List.

The Main Hot List window appears. The page's URL is automatically added to the hot list.

2. Click on the hot list window's close box to close the list.

Moving to a Web page via the hot list

Once you've added a Web page to the hot list, you can quickly move to that page without typing (or remembering) the page's URL.

1. Choose Services⇨Hot Lists. With the mouse button still pressed down, drag the cursor to the right to display a hierarchical menu. Choose Main Hot List from this menu.

The Main Hot List window appears.

2. Double-click on a bookmark from the Main Hot List window.

The AOL browser finds and loads the desired page.

Searching the Web

The AOL browser has a search feature that makes it easy to search for Web pages that pertain to a topic of interest.

1. Choose Services⇨Open URL.

The Uniform Resource Locator window appears.

2. Type **http://webcrawler.com.**

3. Click on the OK button.

You can skip the above steps and instead type the URL **http://webcrawler.com** in the Current URL field of the browser window and then press the Return key. Then move to step 4.

The WebCrawler page appears.

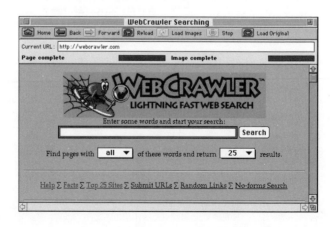

4. Type a word (or words) that describes your interest.

5. Click on the Search button.

The WebCrawler returns a list of Web pages that match your search. Each page mentioned in the list is a hypertext link to that page.

6. Click on a page in the list to go to that page.

The AOL browser loads the desired page.

7. To return to the WebCrawler page, click on the Back arrow icon.

8. To return to the page that you were at prior to using WebCrawler, again click on the Back arrow icon.

 So that you can quickly search the Web during any Web session, add the WebCrawler page to your hot list. ***See also*** "Saving a URL in your hot list," in this section.

Gopher searching from the Web browser

In Part VII you learned how to perform a file-search using America Online's Gopher feature. You can also use Gopher from within the AOL Web browser. Unlike the AOL Gopher resource, the browser version of Gopher offers no Gopher site suggestions — you must know a Gopher server address in order to connect to a server. ***See also*** Appendix A for a list of several Gopher server addresses.

1. Choose Services⇨Gopher.

The Open a Gopher session window appears.

2. Type the address of a Gopher server.

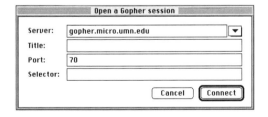

3. Click on the Connect button.

The AOL browser connects to the Gopher server.

4. Double-click on folder and file names until you reach a file of interest. Text files can be read online by double-clicking on them. If a file is a graphics file in the hqx compressed format, you'll be able to save the opened file and uncompress it later. ***See also*** "Uncompressing Downloaded Files" in Part VI.

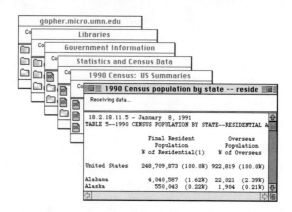

Exiting the AOL Web browser

To exit the browser and return to AOL, choose File⇨Quit.

CompuServe

Most of the commercial online services that support the World Wide Web supply members with a *proprietary* Web browser — software designed to be used exclusively for that online service. For example, the Web browser distributed by America Online won't work from CompuServe. To access the Web, you use an online service's Web browser — and only that browser.

In early 1996, CompuServe will follow a similar, but not identical, path by including their own Web browser in their MacCIM software — the browser will then be *integrated* into the MacCIM program. Until that time — and even after that time — CompuServe members have the option of using any existing Mac Web browsing software. That means that you can use such popular products as Netscape Navigator or MacWeb.

I strongly recommend that CompuServe members use one of the *third party Web browsers* (developed by a software company other than CompuServe), such as Netscape, with CompuServe. *Integrated browsers* like the ones used by some online services — such as America Online — get the job done, but they are often slow and not as feature-packed as browsers developed by outside companies.

To use a browser like Netscape with your CompuServe account, you need to do a few things:

1. Get the files that you need to set up a CompuServe Web connection.

2. Configure your system so that it can bypass the MacCIM software and access the Web by using software such as Netscape Navigator.

3. Obtain a Web browser — preferably for free!

4. Learn how to use the Web browser.

Instead of devoting several pages of this chapter to the details necessary to accomplish the first three points, I've dedicated Appendix E to this purpose (including the how-tos for downloading a free copy of Netscape Navigator). If you aren't currently set up to access the Web via CompuServe, *see* Appendix E now. Then refer back to this part to get the scoop on working with your Netscape Navigator software.

Are you a little nervous about downloading utility files and configuring your system? Don't be! CompuServe turns what could be ugly, tricky tasks into a straightforward process. If you have a CompuServe account, take advantage of the fact that CompuServe allows you to use any number of cool Web browsers — members of other online services don't have that option!

eWorld

The eWorld Web browser provides eWorld members with a very Mac-like way of browsing the World Wide Web.

Obtaining the eWorld Web browser

eWorld doesn't have a built-in Web browser — it uses a separate software program. When you obtained your eWorld software, it might not have come with this Web browser program. eWorld provides this software to eWorld users free of charge — you just need to download it from eWorld. If you don't have an eWorld Web Browser folder in the eWorld folder on your hard drive, follow these steps to get a copy:

1. Click on the Info Booth on the introductory screen.

The Info Booth window appears.

2. Click on the eWorld Up To Date arrow icon.

The eWorld Up To Date window appears.

3. Click on the Latest eWorld Software disk icon.

The Latest eWorld Software window appears.

4. Double-click on the eWorld Application & Web Browser folder (this folder name may have a version number such as 1.1 following the word *eWorld*).

If a window with a message stating that you are entering a Free Area appears, click on the OK button.

The eWorld & Web Browser window appears.

5. Double-click on the eWorld Web Browser folder.

The eWorld Web Browser window appears.

6. Double-click on the eWorld Web Browser name.

A window describing the eWorld Web browser appears.

7. Copy or print the install instructions that appear in the window.

8. Click on the Get File Now button.

eWorld downloads the Web browser to your hard drive.

Starting the eWorld Web browser

Before you can navigate the Web from your eWorld account, you need to start the eWorld Web browser.

1. Connect to eWorld if you haven't already done so.

2. Click on the Internet On-Ramp area of the introductory screen.

The eWorld Internet window appears.

3. Click on the World Wide Web icon.

The World Wide Web window appears.

4. Click on the Enter the World Wide Web button.

If an alert window appears with a message saying that the Web browser couldn't locate the information that you requested, ignore it by clicking on the OK button. Wait a minute or two while eWorld connects to the Web and loads the eWorld home page.

If the browser window doesn't open, choose Service➪Web and wait a minute.

	Apple Welcomes You to the Internet	
🏠 Home	⬅ Back	➡ Forward	🔄 Reload	🖼 Load Images	⏹ Stop	💾 Load Original

Current URL: http://www.eworld.com/inside/

Link URL:

Page complete   **Image complete**

🍎 **WEDNESDAY**

PowerBooks Unmasked
Come here for complete PowerBook info including specifications, capabilities, multimedia support and pre-installed software.

🌐 **Visit eWorld's Web City**

Icons & Clip Art
Bring your work to life with free arrows, flowers, backgrounds, punctuation marks, symbols, bars, dots, cubes, stars & more.

✏️ Go to

Changing the home page

Each time that you start the eWorld Web browser, you find yourself at eWorld's own home page. You can use this as your starting point for navigating the Web, or you can choose any other Web page to be your home page.

1. Choose Edit⇨Configure.

The eWorld Internet Configuration window appears.

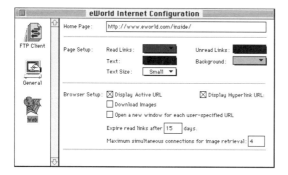

2. Click on the Web icon.

3. Type the URL of the Web page that you want to use as the new home page.

The next time that you connect to the Web and each time thereafter, eWorld will start at the page you entered.

4. Click on the window's close box to close the window.

Following a hypertext link

Hypertext links appear as colored words (or as underlined words) within the rest of a page's text. Icons or pictures that are usually framed may also be links.

1. Click on a hypertext word, icon, or picture to follow that link.

The eWorld browser traverses the Web to find and load the document (page) that the link points to. The Opening connection label near the top of the browser window changes to a Page label. The progress bar to the right of the label indicates the loading progress of the page.

2. Click on the Stop icon if the loading takes too long; otherwise, wait for the page to load.

3. To return to the page you came from, click on the Back arrow icon.

Turning image-loading off

Images that appear on pages (such as pictures and icons) are optional — they add to the Web experience, but they aren't necessary — for viewing the text of a page. If the loading of pages takes too long (usually because your modem is slower than 28.8K), you can set the browser so that it won't load images.

See also Part II for information on modem speeds.

1. Choose Edit⇨Configure.

The eWorld Internet Configuration window appears.

2. Click on the Web icon.

3. Uncheck the Download Images check box.

4. Click on the window's close box to close the window.

5. If the Always Load Images item in the Web menu *is* checked, choose it now to uncheck it.

Web pages that you visit will display a simple, generic icon in place of graphic images. A page that you've already visited during the current session will, however, still display images when you return to that page. That's because the eWorld browser retains this image information and can reload the image quicker than it loads an image it is first encountering.

Turning image-loading on

If you've turned off the image-loading feature and now want to turn image-loading back on, follow these steps:

1. Choose Edit⇨Configure.

The eWorld Internet Configuration window appears.

2. Click on the Web icon.

3. Check the Download Images check box.

4. Click on the window's close box to close the window.

5. If the Always Load Images item in the Web menu *isn't* checked, choose it now to check it.

Moving to a URL

You can click on the Back arrow icon and Forward arrow icon to move to the Web pages that you've just visited. To move to a completely different Web page, follow these steps:

1. Choose Services⇨Open URL.

The Uniform Resource Locator window appears.

2. Type the URL that you wish to move to.

3. Click on the OK button.

The eWorld browser finds and loads the desired page.

Instead of performing the preceding steps, do the following:

1. Highlight the text in the Current URL field of the browser window.

2. Type the URL in that field.

You can also use copy and paste to copy the URL from another window and paste it into the Current URL field.

3. Once you've entered the URL, press the Return key to tell the browser to find and load the page.

Saving a URL in your hot list

If you reach a page that you are interested in and feel that you want to return to that page during another Web session, save the page's URL in your hot list. The *hot list* is the term eWorld uses for an editable list of URLs. (Other Web browsers refer to saved URLs as bookmarks.)

1. With the page displayed in the browser, choose Services⇨Add To Main Hot List.

The Main Hot List window appears. The page's URL is automatically added to the hot list.

2. Click on the hot list window's close box to close the list.

Moving to a Web page via the hot list

Once you've added a Web page to the hot list, you can quickly move to that page without typing (or remembering) the page's URL.

1. Choose Services⇨Hot Lists. With the mouse button still pressed, drag the cursor to the right to display a hierarchical menu. Choose Main Hot List from this menu.

The Main Hot List window appears.

2. Double-click on the bookmark that interests you from the Main Hot List window.

The eWorld browser finds and loads the desired page.

Searching the Web

The eWorld browser has a search feature that makes it easy to search for Web pages that pertain to a topic of interest.

1. Choose Services⇨Open URL.

The Uniform Resource Locator window appears.

2. Type **http://www.online.apple.com/webcity/find/search.html.**

3. Click on the OK button.

You can skip the preceding steps and type the URL **http://www.online.apple.com/webcity/find/search.html** in the Current URL field of the browser window and then press the Return key.

The Find page appears.

4. Type a word (or words) that describes your interest.

5. Click on the Search button.

The search returns a list of Web pages that match your interest — the list is displayed in its own page (the Search Results page). Each name mentioned in the list is a hypertext link to a search result page.

6. Click on a name in the list to go to that page.

The eWorld browser finds and loads the desired page.

7. To return to the search results page, click on the Back arrow icon.

8. To return to the Find page, again click on the Back arrow icon.

9. To return to the page you were at prior to using the Find feature, again click on the Back arrow icon.

So that you can quickly search the Web during any Web session, add the Find page to your hot list. *See also* "Saving a URL in your hot list," in this section.

At the bottom of the Search Results page are several hypertext links to other search pages. If the eWorld search doesn't produce satisfactory results, move to one of the other search pages and try your search again.

Gopher searching from the Web browser

In Part VII, I discuss the Gopher file-searching utility. There, however, I mention that eWorld doesn't offer a Gopher search option. Now's your chance to try your hand at searching Gopherspace — the eWorld Web browser *does* have a Gopher resource. To connect to a Gopher server, you must know a Gopher server address in advance. *See also* Appendix A for a list of several Gopher server addresses.

1. Choose Services➪Gopher.

The Open a Gopher session window appears.

2. Type the address of a Gopher server.

3. Click on the Connect button.

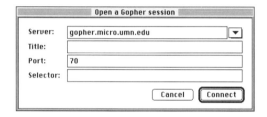

The eWorld browser connects to the Gopher server.

4. Double-click on folder and file names until you reach a file that interests you.

Text files can be read online by double-clicking on them. If a file

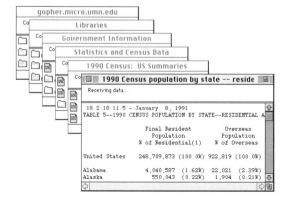

is a graphics file in the hqx compressed format, you can save the opened file and uncompress it later. ***See also*** "Uncompressing Downloaded Files," in Part VI.

Exiting the eWorld Web browser

To exit the browser and return to eWorld, select File⇨Quit.

Netscape Navigator

Netscape Navigator is a Web browser often included in the Internet access software packages supplied by local Internet access providers

Obtaining the Netscape Navigator Web browser

If you don't already have Netscape Navigator, you can get a free copy by signing onto CompuServe, visiting an FTP site, and downloading it. ***See*** Appendix E for all the details.

Starting the Netscape Navigator Web browser

✦ If you have Netscape as part of a package of Internet software provided by a local access carrier, then you should start Netscape as instructed in the documentation that your carrier sent you.

✦ If you're software package is managed from a palette of icons, you typically click on one icon to connect to the Internet and then click on the Netscape icon to start the Netscape software.

✦ If you're using Netscape from a CompuServe account, don't sign on to CompuServe. Instead, make sure that you're not connected to CompuServe. Set up your CompuServe account as specified in Appendix E. Then, whenever you double-click on the Netscape Navigator icon from the desktop, Navigator launches and automatically connects to the Web.

No matter how you start Netscape, the end result is the same — Netscape connects to the Web and then takes a minute to load the information from its own home page.

Changing the home page

Each time that you run the Netscape browser, you find yourself at Netscape's own home page. You can use this home page as your starting point for navigating the Web, or you can choose any other Web page to be your home page.

1. Choose Options⇨Preferences.

The Preferences window appears.

2. Choose Window and Link Styles from the pop-up menu at the top of the window.

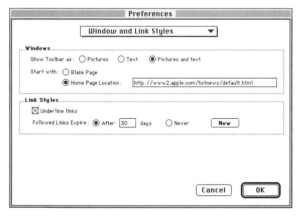

3. In the Home Page Location field, type the URL of the Web page that you want to use as the new home page.

4. Click on the OK button.

The next time that you connect to the Web — and each time thereafter — Netscape will start at the page you entered.

Following a hypertext link

Hypertext links appear as colored words (or as underlined words) within the rest of a page's text. Icons or pictures that are usually framed may also be links.

1. Click on a hypertext word, icon, or picture to follow that link.

The Netscape browser traverses the Web to find and then load the document (page) that the link points to. The progress bar located at the bottom right of the browser window indicates the loading progress of the page.

2. Click on the Stop icon if the loading takes too long; otherwise, wait for the page to load.

3. To return to the page that you came from, click on the Back arrow icon.

Turning image-loading off

Images that appear on pages (such as pictures and icons) are optional — they add to the Web experience, but they aren't necessary — for viewing the text of a page. If the loading takes too long (usually because your modem is slower than 28.8K) you can set the browser so that it won't load images:

1. Click on the Options menu and look at the Auto Load Image item

If the Auto Load Image item is unchecked, the image-loading feature is already turned off.

2. If Auto Load Image is checked, choose it to uncheck it.

Web pages that you visit will display a simple, generic icon in place of graphic images. A page that you've already visited during this session will, however, still display images when you return to that page. The Netscape browser retains this image information and can reload the image quicker than it loads an image it is first encountering.

Turning image-loading on

If you've turned off the image-loading feature and now want to turn image-loading back on, choose Options⇨Auto Load Image to check that item.

Moving to a URL

You can click on the Back arrow icon and Forward arrow icon to move to the Web pages that you just visited. To move to a completely different Web page, follow these steps:

1. Choose File⇨Open Location.

The Open Location window appears.

2. Type the URL that you wish to move to.

3. Click on the Open button.

   The Netscape browser finds and loads the desired page.

Here is an even faster way:

1. Highlight the text in the Netsite field of the browser window.

2. Type the URL in that field.

   You can also use copy and paste to copy the URL from another window and paste it into the Current URL field.

3. Once you've entered the URL, press the Return key to tell the browser to find and load the page.

Saving a URL via the Bookmarks menu

If you reach an interesting page and feel that you will want to return to this page during another Web session, save the page's URL as a *bookmark* — a reference to a Web page. Once the current page is saved as a bookmark, you can quickly return to that same page at any time — during your current Web session or any other time you browse the Web.

Netscape stores bookmarks in the Bookmarks menu. To create a bookmark for the current Web page, choose Bookmarks⇨Add Bookmark. The following figure shows a Bookmarks menu with four bookmarks.

Moving to a Web page via the Bookmarks menu

Once you've created a bookmark for a Web page, you can return to that page any time by choosing the page's bookmark from the

Bookmarks menu. Once you do that, the Netscape browser finds and loads the desired page.

Changing a bookmark's name

When you create a bookmark, Netscape gives the bookmark a name. That name then appears as a menu item in the Bookmarks menu. If the bookmark name isn't as descriptive as you'd like, change it:

1. Choose Bookmarks⇨View Bookmarks.

The Bookmark List window appears.

2. Click once on the bookmark that you want in the window's list.

3. Type a new bookmark name in the Name box.

4. Click on the window's close box when you are finished.

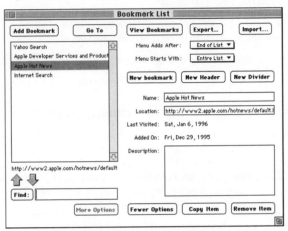

Rearranging bookmarks in the Bookmarks menu

If you aren't satisfied with the order in which bookmarks appear in the Bookmarks window, you can rearrange them:

1. Choose Bookmarks⇨View Bookmarks.

The Bookmark List window appears.

2. Click once on the bookmark in the window's list.

3. Click on the up or down arrow button located beneath the list to move the item up or down one place in the list.

4. Repeat step 3 to move a bookmark further up or down in the list

5. Click on the window's close box when you are finished.

Removing a bookmark from the Bookmarks menu

If you'd like to remove a bookmark from the Bookmarks menu, follow these steps:

1. Choose Bookmarks⇨View Bookmarks.

The Bookmark List window appears.

2. Click once on the bookmark that interests you in the window's list.

3. Click on the Remove Item button.

4. Click on the window's close box when you are finished.

Searching the Web

The Netscape browser makes it easy to search for Web pages that pertain to a topic of interest.

1. Click on the Net Search button in the browser window.

The Netscape Search page appears in the browser window.

2. Type a word or words that describes your interest.

3. Click on the Search button.

The infoseek guide displays a new Search Results page that holds a list of Web pages that match your search. Each page mentioned in the list is a hypertext link to that page.

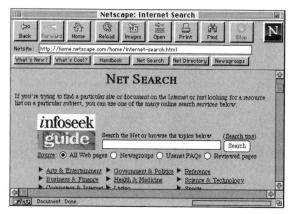

4. Click on a page in the list to go to that page.

The Netscape browser finds and loads the desired page.

5. To return to search results page, click on the Back arrow icon.

6. To return to the Netscape Search page, again click on the Back arrow icon.

7. To return to the page that you were at prior to using the Netscape search page, again click on the Back arrow icon.

The Netscape search page offers a host of *search engines* — different means of searching the Web. Scroll down the search page to see the other offerings. If a Web page of interest doesn't materialize from your first search, try one of these other types of searches — each works in way similar to the search engine that appears at the top of the search page.

Prodigy

If you're a Mac user with a Prodigy account and hope to browse the World Wide Web, you're out of luck — at least at the time of this writing. Prodigy has a Web browser integrated into its Windows software, but the Mac version isn't complete yet. When the Mac version is complete, it should have a look similar to the Web browsers used by most online services — in general, that means a window with an edit box that allows you to type in a URL.

Because the Prodigy Mac Web browser is incomplete at the time of this writing, the following instructions are subject to change.

Starting the Prodigy Web browser

The Prodigy Web browser will be integrated into the Prodigy software — it won't be a separate application. To enter the Web, follow these steps:

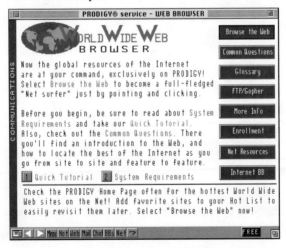

1. Connect to Prodigy if you haven't already done so.

2. Click on the small Web button at the bottom of the Prodigy window.

The World Wide Web window appears.

3. Click on the Browse the Web button.

The Web Browser window appears. After a delay of up to a minute or so, the Prodigy home page is displayed in the window.

Following a hypertext link

Hypertext links appear as colored words (or as underlined words) within the rest of a page's text. Icons or pictures that are usually framed may also be links.

1. Click on a hypertext word, icon, or picture to follow that link.

The Prodigy browser traverses the Web to find and then load the document (page) that the link points to. Allow time for the page to be loaded.

2. To return to the page you came from, click on the Back arrow icon.

Moving to a URL

To move to a different Web page, you need to know that page's URL (Uniform Resource Locator) — its address. An example is the address of one of Apple's own Web pages, `http://www.apple.com`. To move to a new page, do the following:

1. Type the URL to connect to in the Document URL box of the Web browser window.

2. Press the Enter key.

The Prodigy Web browser finds and loads the requested page.

Part IX

Doing Business on the Internet

The Internet used to be the domain of the universities and government agencies. Businesses played a role in the Net — but nothing like they do now or will in the future. Starting in 1994, the number of Web pages devoted to business increased dramatically. More than any other part of the Internet, it will be the Web that attracts business. That's because the Web allows for graphics — an important part of catching the interest of potential customers.

In this part . . .

- ✔ HTML — the language of the Web page
- ✔ Creating your own Web page
- ✔ Posting your Web page to a server
- ✔ Getting your Web page noticed

Setting Up a Web Site

Businesses big and small are jumping onto the Web. You can, too. In the last year, Web page creation has become much easier — and cheaper.

HTML: The language of the Web

HTML, or HyperText Markup Language, is the formatting language used to design Web pages. Using a standard format for all Web pages allows Web browsers to exist — if a Web browser can interpret the formatting of one Web page, it can understand the formatting of any page.

A Web browser and an Internet server communicate by means of a second standard — HTTP. *HTTP* is the HyperText Transfer Protocol, and it is the reason you type `http` at the start of every URL (Uniform Resource Locator). ***See also*** "Uniform Resource Locators (URLs)," in Part VIII of this book.

To create your own Web page, you need to learn HTML. Several books and free documents can help you reach your goal to learn HTML. You can find links to several documents on one of Netscape's Web pages:

```
http://www.netscape.com/assist/net_sites/index.html
```

Once you know the language, you don't need any fancy or expensive software tools — an inexpensive *text editor* (a simplified word processor) capable of saving a document as an HTML document is all you need.

After your HTML document is complete, it needs to be placed on a Web server. Because Web servers use expensive high-speed communication lines, individuals and small businesses don't typically place their pages directly on a Web server. Instead, they rent space on the server of a larger business that has been set up for just that purpose.

In summary, to create a Web page you need to do the following:

1. Learn the HyperText Markup Language.

2. Use a text editor to create your HTML document.

3. Place your HTML document on a Web server.

As you see in the next section, steps 1 and 2 can be combined into a single step — one that makes things much easier for you.

If there's an easier way, why bother learning HTML? Because HTML is more powerful than the graphical tools you're going to read about. If your page is to be a simple one, use a graphical tool. If it is going to be complex, you'll want to know the HTML language.

Graphical Web page authoring tools

For many people, learning a new language like HTML doesn't sound like much fun. If you fit that bill, then you'll want to consider using a software package that uses a point-and-click interface to piece together a Web page document. After you've assembled the document, this type of software does the necessary conversion to make it a true HTML document — one that is accepted by a Web server.

The PageMill solution

Adobe's PageMill is currently the favorite graphical authoring package. PageMill costs about $100. That $100 could be considered money well spent if you aren't the type whose interested in learning the intricacies of a new language.

The Navisoft solution

America Online is known for making things simple for its millions of members. It made things simple initially with its very user-friendly AOL software, and it did it again with its Web browser. So it should come as no surprise that America Online now offers an "all in one" Web page solution.

Navisoft, an AOL-owned company, lets you download free software for creating a Web page. After you create your document, you can again use the services of Navisoft to post your Web page — for free. There's a catch of course — it's free for only a trial period. If, after the period is up, you're satisfied with the results, you can choose to keep your Web page posted and pay Navisoft a monthly fee. A simple Web page costs about $20 per month. You can get more information about Navisoft and its NaviService by visiting its own Web page at `http://www.naviservice.com`.

Getting Your Page Noticed

Creating a Web page for your own business is only half the battle. Now you've got to make people aware of the fact that your page exists. Since you'll be competing with *millions* of other Web pages, perhaps this task represents more than half the battle.

Yahoo and WebLaunch

You've encountered the Yahoo Web-searching site at a few places in this book. Recall that, by going to the Web page at `http://www.yahoo.com`, you can enter a keyword, or keywords, and perform a Web page search. The results returned by Yahoo are links to all the Web pages that match your search criteria.

Getting your Web page listed in a *search engine* seems like a great way to make your page known — and it is. But wait — it gets better. Yahoo lets you add your page to its massive index of Web pages for no charge! The following figure shows a part of the online form used to add a page. To get to this form

1. Go to the Yahoo page at `http://www.yahoo.com`.

2. Click on the Add URL text in the Yahoo logo picture, or you can type in the URL shown in this figure:

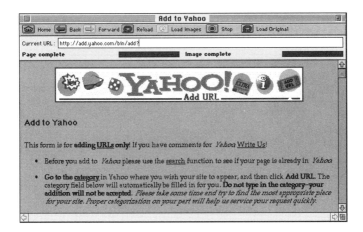

Yahoo offers one additional service that really helps get your page noticed. For a fee of $750 dollars, Yahoo will *billboard* your site at the busiest locations on the Web for one week. That is, Yahoo will display a graphic advertisement and a hypertext link to your page on several popular pages. After the week is up, your page gets a high-profile place in the Yahoo Web index.

AAA Internet Promotions

Yahoo isn't the only search facility on the Web. A Web-publicity company named AAA Internet Promotions takes advantage of this fact by offering to place your URL in a collection of more than 50 indexes currently available on the Web. You can get more information about AAA Internet Promotions by visiting their Web page at `http://www.west.net/~solution`.

Gopher Servers of Interest

To perform a gopher search, you need the address of a gopher server. If your Internet access software provides you with one or more Gopher sites, you're all set. If not, look here.

Gopher Server Addresses

To find information by browsing Internet files using Gopher, you need the address of a Gopher server. That's your starting point. After you connect to a server, you move about from folder-to-folder, gopher server-to-gopher server, by clicking the mouse. Start with any one of the Gopher sites listed below.

If your Internet service fails to connect with a server, just try another from the list. Don't get discouraged — Gopher servers are known to be somewhat fussy.

Address	Description
gopher.micro.umn.edu	University of Minnesota; this gopher site may have all the information you need
gopher.ohiolink.edu	Several Ohio University libraries
gopher.unc.edu	University of North Carolina
gopher.use.edu	University of Southern California
gopher.virginia.edu	University of Virginia
gopher.well.sf.ca.us	A gopher located in San Francisco, *well* stands for the *Whole Earth 'Lectronic Library*
yaleinfo.yale.edu	Yale library

Archie Servers and FTP Sites of Interest

To perform an Archie search for a file to FTP, you need the address of an Archie server. Some Archie *clients* (software for connecting to an Archie server) come preconfigured with the addresses of several Archie sites. If you don't have such a handy Archie client, choose one of the server addresses from this appendix.

A few FTP sites are so loaded with Mac files that you might not need to do any kind of Internet search at all — you can just head to one of them and browse through its Mac folders until you find a file of interest. You'll find the addresses of several such FTP sites on the following pages.

Archie Server Addresses

If you're looking for a particular file and you know its name (or part of its name) and your Internet provider allows you to perform an Archie search, you'll need the address of an Archie server. If you fail to connect to one (Archie servers can get overloaded with users like yourself), just try a different one.

◆ archie.ans.net
◆ archie.internic.net
◆ archie.rutgers.edu
◆ archie.sura.net
◆ archie.unl.edu

FTP Addresses

Thousands of FTP servers are connected to the Internet, so you won't be surprised to learn that the following list isn't comprehensive! It does, however, provide a good sampling of sites of interest to Mac users.

1. Use your FTP software (whether your FTP software is built into your commercial online software or you use a separate program like Fetch) to connect to one of the following FTP sites.

2. Then double-click your way into the folder shown in the right column of the following table.

For better luck connecting to any of these FTP servers, try to make your connection during evening hours — with businesses closed, you'll only be vying with individual users such as yourself for a connection.

Address	Directory to Visit
sumex-aim.standford.edu	/info-mac
ftp.ucs.ubc.ca	/pub/mac/info-mac
mac.archive.umich.edu	/mac
ftp.apple.com	/dts
ftp.ncsa.uiuc.edu	/Mac
ftp.funet.fi	/pub/mac
ftp.dartmouth.edu	/pub/mac
boombox.micro.umn.edu	/pub

Web Pages of Interest

To browse a Web page, you need the URL of that page. This appendix lists several — which should be more than enough to keep you busy surfin' the Net!

Web Pages

With your Web browser up and running, type one of the following addresses into the box that accepts a URL in the browser window.

http://www.apple.com

This is Apple's own Web page. Here, you'll find hypertext links that lead to pages that provide information about Apple and its products, support for users of Apple software and hardware, and support for those interested in programming the Macintosh.

http://galaxy.einet.net

Here, you'll find a wealth of information on just about any topic: business, commerce, engineering, government, law, recreation, medicine, or science. Want to know about holistic medicine? motorcycles? music? With Galaxy's well laid-out hypertext links, it's all just a mouse-click away.

http://www.commerce.net

CommerceNet is a huge business society with its base in Silicon Valley. It's a nonprofit corporation designed to test technologies that support electronic commerce over the Internet.

http://rever.nmsu.edu/~elharo

The individual who runs this Web page calls this page the Well Connected Mac page. It is. This page has hypertext links to all sorts of information and software useful to Mac enthusiasts. Check out the Macintosh FAQ lists link to see a number of Frequently Asked Questions lists (with answers, of course).

http://www.yahoo.com

Can't find a Web page that has the information you seek? *URL* on over to this Web-searching page. This page is one of — if not the — most comprehensive index of other Web sites. Type in a search word and click the Search button to get a list of hypertext links to jump to.

http://www.metrowerks.com

You already know how to use the Mac, right? Now, are you interested in learning how to *program* it, too? If so, check out this Web page. It's the home of Metrowerks, the company that develops and sells the hottest Macintosh development tools — for rookie or advanced programmers alike.

http://lcewww.et.tudelft.nl/people/vdham/info-mac

Info-mac digests are electronic journals that represent a prime
resource for all types of Macintosh information. This Web page has
hypertext links to the most current issues, as well as hundreds of
back issues.

http://hyperarchive.lcs.mit.edu/HyperArchive.html

This site provides brief descriptions of numerous Mac files — a useful
feature that saves you the time of downloading something that isn't
really of interest to you.

Noteworthy Newsgroups

Newsgroups are popular because they offer something for everyone — there are *thousands* of them. This appendix lists several newsgroups. Use your Internet access software to drop in on a few and check out the messages that are posted within. If you find a group of interest, add it to your list of saved newsgroups.

Animal Interests

Name	Discussion
alt.animals.badgers	Yes, really — discussion about badgers
alt.animals.dolphins	Flipper and friends
alt.aquaria	Tropical fish enthusiasts
alt.pets.rabbits	Rabbit lovers
alt.wolves	Wolves and wolf-dog mixes

Comedy

Name	Discussion
alt.comedy.british	British comedy discussions
alt.comedy.standup	Stand-up comedy and comedians
alt.comedy.monty-python	Monty Python's Flying Circus

Computer Users

Name	Discussion
alt.bbs.internet	Bulletin board services that are connected to the Internet
alt.lang.basic	The BASIC computer language
alt.online-service.america-online	Questions and answers about America Online
alt.online-service.compuserve	Questions and answers about CompuServe
alt.online-service.prodigy	Questions and answers about Prodigy
alt.sources.mac	Source code file examples for programmers

Fan Clubs

Name	Discussion
alt.books.anne-rice	Vampires and Anne Rice
alt.elvis.king	Need I say more?
alt.fan.blues-brothers	Jake and Elwood
alt.fan.howard-stern	The radio and TV "personality"
alt.fan.letterman	David Letterman
alt.fan.u2	The Irish rockers
alt.woody-allen	The actor/director

Games

Name	Discussion
alt.anagrams	Word games
alt.games.mtrek	Multi-Trek, the multiuser Star Trek-style game
alt.games.video.classic	Pong, anyone?
alt.sega.genesis	Sega fans
alt.super.nes	Super NES fans

Religion

Name	Discussion
alt.christnet	For Christians
alt.christnet.bible	Bible discussion and research
alt.christnet.philosophy	Philosophical stuff
alt.hindu	For Hindus
alt.philosophy.zen	Zen discussions
alt.religion.islam	Islamic discussions

Sports

Name	Discussion
alt.archery	Archery discussions
alt.fishing	The one that got away
alt.skate-board	All about skateboarding
alt.sport.bowling	In the gutter—yet somehow still clean — discussions
alt.sport.darts	Dart discussions
alt.sport.pool	Billiard talk
alt.sports.football.pro.gb-packers	Green Bay Packers fans
alt.surfing	Riding the waves

CompuServe and Web Browsing Software

If you're a member of CompuServe, you have the luxury of using the Web browser of your choice to access the World Wide Web. That's something that can't be said of most other commercial online services. This appendix shows you how to get set up.

CompuServe and the Web

Unlike most online services, CompuServe lets you use just about any available Mac Web browsing software to browse the Web. To take advantage of this nice feature, you need to perform a few one-time-only steps. In this appendix, you'll see how to do the following:

✦ Get the files you need to set up a CompuServe Web connection

✦ *Easily* configure your system so that it can bypass the MacCIM software and access the Web using software such as Netscape Navigator

✦ Use your existing CompuServe account to download a *free* copy of the Macintosh version of the very popular Netscape Navigator software

✦ Connect to the Web using Netscape Navigator

See also Part VIII and read about using the Netscape Navigator Web browser.

Connecting to the Web: Getting Started

Getting your CompuServe account set up for Web access is easy — yet this appendix is several pages long. Don't be put off by its length! Many of the following pages contain only a few sentences that pertain to you — they describe situations such as "If you have this type of Mac, do this. If you have that type of Mac, do that." Essentially, you'll be doing only the following tasks to get your account ready:

✦ Getting a copy of the MacTCP control and placing it in the Control Panels folder of the System Folder on your Mac.

✦ Getting a copy of the PPP system extension and placing it in the Extensions folder of the System Folder on your Mac.

✦ Getting a copy of the Config PPP control and placing it in the Control Panels folder of the System Folder on your Mac.

✦ Getting a copy of a utility program named CompuServe PPP Utility and running it to let it handle all of the system configuration details for you — without any input from you!

This appendix also tells you the FTP server address to go to from your CompuServe account if you're interested in downloading a free copy of the Netscape Navigator browser.

Finally, this appendix ends by telling you how to access the Web. I'll give the secret away right here and now — after your system is configured, all you need to do is double-click on the Netscape Navigator icon to get connected!

Enough rhetoric — it's time to get connected!

To get started, you need a few communications files. The next few sections tell you how to go about getting them. If you own a Power Mac (a Macintosh that has a PowerPC chip) read the next section — "Getting MacTCP for Power Macintosh." If you have what's simply called a Macintosh (a Mac that has a 68K chip like the 68030 or 68040), skip the next section and move on to "Getting MacTCP for the Macintosh."

Getting MacTCP for Power Macintosh

If the word *PowerPC* appears on the case of your Macintosh computer, you have a Power Macintosh — you should read this section. If not, skip to the next section — "Getting MacTCP for the Macintosh."

MacTCP is a software utility widely distributed by Apple — you might already have It In your System Folder. To check

1. Take a look in the Control Panels folder of your System Folder.

If the MacTCP control panel is there, then you're all set.

2. Skip the rest of this "Getting MacTCP for Power Macintosh" section and jump to the "Getting the CompuServe PPP Utility program" section.

If you don't have MacTCP in your Control Panels folder, don't worry — you still have the file. You'll find it on your system installation disks or CD. It just didn't happen to be one of the files that got installed onto your hard drive when the System Folder was put there.

Your Power Macintosh came with either a single system software CD or a set of system software disks. To find the MacTCP file, follow these steps to perform a search on the system CD or system disks:

1. Place the system software CD or one of the system software disks in your Mac's drive.

2. Choose File⇨Find.

The Find File window appears.

3. Choose the CD or disk from the pop-up menu that appears to the right of the Find items label.

4. Type **mactcp**.

5. Click on the Find button.

The Items Found window appears. If you're searching your system CD, go to step 6 now. If you're searching a system disk rather than a system CD, the file might not be on the disk that you're currently searching. If that's the case, eject the disk and insert a different system disk in the drive. Repeat steps 3 through 5. If you do this with each disk, eventually you'll find the file!

6. Click once on the MacTCP icon in the Items Found window.

The folder path to the file appears in the bottom of the window. This figure provides an example of what your folder path *might* look like:

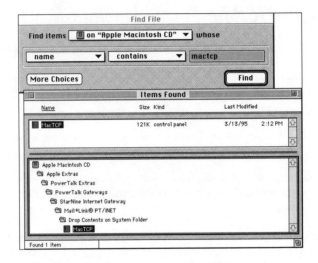

7. Using the Items Found window as your guide, open folders on the system CD or disk until you come to the MacTCP file.

8. Drag the MacTCP file to the *closed* System Folder on your hard drive and release the mouse button.

An alert window opens telling you that this file must go in the Control Panels folder.

9. Click on the OK button.

You've just added the MacTCP file to the Control Panels folder of your System Folder. Now skip the next section and move on to the "Getting the CompuServe PPP Utility Program" section.

Getting MacTCP for the Macintosh

MacTCP is a software utility widely distributed by Apple — you may already have a copy of it. Look in the Control Panels folder of your System Folder to see if a copy of the MacTCP control panel is there. If it is, then you're all set — you can skip the rest of this "Getting MacTCP for the Macintosh" section and *see* the "Getting MacPPP" section.

If you *don't* have MacTCP in your Control Panels folder, don't worry — you might still have the file. If you have System 7.5, you'll find it on your system installation CD or disks. MacTCP just didn't happen to be one of the files installed onto your hard drive when the System Folder was put there.

If you *don't* have MacTCP in your Control Panels folder and you *do* have System 7.5, perform these steps to get MacTCP added to your Control Panels folder:

1. Run the system Installer program from your system software CD or system software disks by double-clicking on its icon.

An introductory window appears.

2. Click on the Continue button.

The System 7.5 Installation window appears.

3. Click on the Easy Install pop-up menu and choose Custom Install.

4. Click on the small arrow icon to the left of the Networking Software check box.

5. Click on the MacTCP check box to check it.

6. Click on the Install button.

If an alert window appears with a message telling you that installation cannot take place while other applications are running, click on the Continue button.

The installer finds the MacTCP control panel on your system software CD or disks and adds it to your Control Panels folder in your System Folder.

7. When an alert window appears with a message telling you that installation was successful, click on the Restart button to shutdown and then restart your Macintosh.

If you have System 7.5, you're done with this section — now move on to the "Getting the CompuServe PPP Utility Program" section.

If you have a version of System 7 that came out prior to System 7.5, you probably won't find MacTCP in your Control Panels folder and you won't find it on your system software CD or disks. You can, however, purchase MacTCP from your Apple dealer. Don't run out and do that just yet, though. Instead, consider getting IDG's *Internet For Macs For Dummies Starter Kit*. Besides getting a very helpful book about the Internet, you get a couple of disks that include several programs and utilities — one of which just happens to be MacTCP.

Getting the CompuServe PPP Utility Program

Configuring the MacTCP and MacPPP utilities is normally a task that's a little tricky. So CompuServe has developed a small, *very* easy-to-use program named *CompuServe PPP Utility* that does *all* the work for you. The program is available for downloading from CompuServe. To download that program, follow these steps:

1. Log on to CompuServe if you haven't already.

2. Double-click on the Internet icon in the Browse window.

The Internet window appears.

3. Click on the World Wide Web icon.

The World Wide Web window appears.

4. Double-click on the Download CompuServe Software icon.

The CompuServe Software & Products window appears.

5. Double-click on the CompuServe PPP Utility (Macintosh) icon.

The CompuServe Software window appears.

6. Double-click on the Download CompuServe PPP Utility icon.

A CISPPP.SEA download window appears.

7. Click on the Retrieve icon.

The standard Save window appears.

8. Click on the Save button.

CompuServe downloads the file to your hard drive.

Don't disconnect from CompuServe just yet. You've got one more file to download — the MacPPP file. *See also* "Getting the MacPPP File" in this part.

Getting the MacPPP File

MacPPP is a software utility that allows you to make what's called a *PPP* (Point-to-Point Protocol) connection to the Internet. (You don't need to know the details about this type of connection — you need to know only that this is the type of connection you make when you use CompuServe to access the Web.) To use graphical Internet software like Netscape and TurboGopher with CompuServe, you need this type of connection.

Downloading MacPPP

MacPPP is free from CompuServe. You can download a copy by following these steps:

1. If the CompuServe Software & Products window is still open from your download of the CompuServe PPP Utility program, skip to step 6.

2. Log on to CompuServe if you aren't still connected.

3. Double-click on the Internet icon in the Browse window.

The Internet window appears.

4. Click on the World Wide Web icon.

The World Wide Web window appears.

5. Double-click on the Download CompuServe Software icon.

The CompuServe Software & Products window appears.

6. Double-click on the CompuServe PPP Utility (Macintosh) icon.

The CompuServe Software window appears.

7. Double-click on the Download MacPPP icon.

A MACPPP.SIT download window appears.

8. Click on the Retrieve icon.

The standard Save window appears.

9. Click on the Save button.

MacCIM downloads the file to your hard drive.

10. Choose File⇨Quit to disconnect from CompuServe and exit MacCIM.

A window appears asking if you want to uncompress down-loaded files. If the check box for the MacPPP file *isn't* checked, click on it to check it.

11. Click on the Decompress button.

The standard Save file window appears.

12. Click on the Unstuff button.

MacCIM unstuffs the file. A window appears asking if you have other files to unstuff.

13. Click on the Done button.

Moving MacPPP to your System Folder

The MacPPP file is a *system software extension* — a file that adds functionality to your system folder. That means it belongs in the Extensions folder found in your System Folder. Take these steps to move it to that folder:

1. If you *do* have a MacPPP 2.01 (or similar) folder on your hard drive, then you *did* successfully unstuff the MacPPP file when you quit MacCIM. Go to step 2 now.

If you *don't* have a MacPPP folder on your hard drive, then you *didn't* unstuff the MacPPP 2.01.sit file when you quit MacCIM. You need to do that now. Find the downloaded MacPPP file on your hard drive. It will have the name MacPPP 2.01.sit or something similar (the version number may be different, for instance). Double-click on the MacPPP 2.01.sit file now to unstuff it.

2. You no longer need the stuffed MacPPP 2.01.sit file, so drag it to the Trash.

3. Open the MacPPP folder, select the PPP file, and drag it to the *closed* System Folder and release the mouse button.

An alert window opens telling you that this file must go in the Extensions folder.

4. Click on the OK button.

5. Drag the Config PPP file from the MacPPP folder to the *closed* System Folder and release the mouse button.

An alert window opens telling you that this file must go in the Control Panels folder.

6. Click on the OK button.

Getting the Netscape Navigator Web Browser

You can get Netscape Navigator free by connecting to the Internet and using FTP to download a copy.

1. Connect to CompuServe using MacCIM, as you've always done in the past.

2. Double-click on the Internet icon in the Browse window.

The Internet window appears.

3. Click on the File Downloads (FTP) icon.

You might be faced with a window that lets you know that CompuServe is not responsible for the quality of files housed on FTP servers.

The File Transfer Protocol window appears.

4. Click on the Access a Specific Site icon.

The Access a Specific Site window appears.

5. Type **ftp.netscape.com** in the Site Name box.

6. Click on the OK button.

CompuServe connects you to the Netscape FTP server, and an introductory window appears.

7. Click on the OK button.

8. If you get a busy message, repeat steps 4 through 7, this time using one of the other Netscape FTP site addresses in step 5: `ftp.netscape1.com`, or `ftp.netscape2.com`, or `ftp.netscape3.com`.

9. Double-click on the `netscape` directory in the Directories list.

10. Double-click on the `mac` directory in the Directories list.

11. Click on the check box that appears to the left of the NETSCAPE-1.12.HQX file name.

If the list has a later version of the Netscape file, you can instead check its check box.

12. Click on the Retrieve button.

A standard Save window appears.

13. Click on the Save button.

CompuServe downloads the file to your hard drive.

A file that has a .hqx extension needs to be uncompressed. Use either StuffIt Expander or Compact Pro to uncompress the downloaded file. The results reveal a fully functional version of Netscape Navigator!

Preparing the Communications Files

Configuring files sounds tough. Thankfully, CompuServe has made this task relatively painless. Before configuring the files (adjusting settings within them), you need to get everything prepared by moving the files to their correct locations on your hard drive.

1. Quit MacCIM if you haven't already done so.

2. Make sure that the MacTCP control panel is in your Control Panels folder in the System Folder. If it's not, *see* either the "Getting MacTCP for the Macintosh" or "Getting MacTCP for Power Macintosh" section for instructions.

3. Make sure that the Config PPP control panel is in your Control Panels folder in the System Folder. If it's not, *see* the "Getting MacPPP" section for instructions.

4. Make sure that the PPP extension is in your Extensions folder in the System Folder. If it's not, *see* the "Getting MacPPP" section for instructions.

5. Find the downloaded utility file on your hard drive.

Look for the name CompuServe PPP Utility.sea or something similar.

6. Double-click on the file to extract the CompuServe PPP Utility program from this self-extracting archive file.

7. You no longer need the compressed CompuServe PPP Utility.sea file, so drag it to the Trash.

8. Double-click on the CompuServe PPP Utility icon to launch the program.

The CompuServe PPP Utility window appears.

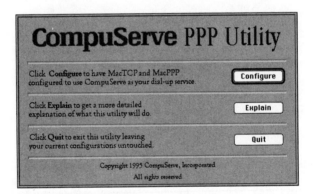

9. Click on the Configure button.

The program quickly configures the MacTCP and PPP utilities for you. An alert window appears with a message telling you that the configuration was successful.

10. Click on the Restart button to shutdown and then restart your Macintosh.

Your Mac is now all set up for Web access — you won't have to repeat *any* of the previous steps from this appendix. Instead, you simply run your Web browsing software and it automatically connects to the Web via CompuServe. If you don't have a Web browser, read the preceding section to see how to get a free copy of the Netscape Navigator browser. If you already have Netscape, skip to the "Starting the Netscape Navigator Web Browser" section now.

Starting the Netscape Navigator Web Browser

You don't browse the Web by signing on to CompuServe with MacCIM. Instead, make sure that you're *not* running MacCIM. Then just double-click on the Netscape Navigator icon. You'll see the following window:

After a couple of minutes or less, the window disappears — if it doesn't, you've encountered some sort of connection error:

1. Click on the Quit button.

2. Then choose File⇨Quit to exit Navigator.

3. Turn your modem off and then back on.

4. Now try running the Netscape Navigator program again.

After a short time, you see the Netscape window open, and you are connected to the World Wide Web. To learn how to browse the Web using Netscape Navigator, *see* Part VIII.

Techie Talk

address

Internet users have an address to which e-mail is sent by other Internet users.

America Online (AOL)

A commercial online service. The software used to access both AOL and the Internet takes full advantage of the Mac interface, making AOL a very popular service with nontechnical users. With over four million members as of the end of 1995, AOL is the leader among online services — with CompuServe a close second.

Anarchie

Commercial online services come with access software that has built-in FTP searching features. Local online services provide members with a combination of software programs for various tasks such as FTP file searching. Anarchie (pronounced *anarchy,* not *an archie*) is one of the more popular FTP search programs included in Internet software packages. Anarchie performs **Archie** searches of the Internet.

anonymous FTP

To download a file from a computer on the Internet, you use a transfer method named FTP. To access a computer on the Internet for the purpose of copying a file using FTP, you need to enter a password. Many Internet computers allow unrestricted copying of their files by allowing users to simply use the word *anonymous* as the password.

Archie

A means of searching the Internet for files of interest. Once found, a file can be **downloaded** to your Mac using **FTP**.

article

A **message** in a newsgroup.

binary file

A file that contains more than text. Examples are a file that holds a picture, a file that holds a sound, or a software program.

browser

A software program used to view World Wide Web **pages**. Also called a Web browser.

CompuServe (CIS)

A commercial online service. With a membership just topping four million at the end of 1995, CompuServe ranks a close second to America Online in number of users. When CompuServe's MacCIM software is used to access CompuServe and the Internet, members enjoy a graphical interface that is very Mac-like.

.cpt

The file extension for a file that has been compressed with the program Compact Pro. Either Compact Pro or the program StuffIt Expander can be used to uncompress such a file.

download

The copying, or transferring, of a file from a computer on the Internet or a commercial online service computer to your own Macintosh computer.

e-mail

Electronic mail. A message that is sent from the computer of one person to the computer of another person.

electronic mail

See **e-mail**.

Eudora

Commercial online services come with access software that has built-in e-mail features. Local online services provide members with a combination of software programs for various tasks such as working with e-mail. Eudora is one of the more popular e-mail programs included in Internet software packages.

eWorld

Apple's own commercial online service. In terms of members, eWorld can't boast anywhere near the same numbers as America Online and CompuServe. However, eWorld is nonetheless a popular service with Macintosh users. While both the Internet and the Web can be accessed from eWorld software, 1996 will see an even greater emphasis on the Net.

Fetch

Commercial online services come with access software that has a built-in **FTP** feature. Local online services provide members with a combination of software programs for various tasks such as using FTP to download files from the Internet. Fetch is one of the more popular FTP programs included in Internet software packages.

file-transfer protocol

The means for downloading, or transferring, a file from an Internet computer to your Macintosh computer. Also referred to as **FTP**.

flame

To post an angry, often insulting, message to a **newsgroup** or another member of the Internet community. In short, be nice — don't flame!

FTP (File Transfer Protocol)

A method for transferring, or downloading, a file from a computer on the Internet to your own Macintosh computer.

Gopher

A file-browsing resource that is useful for moving about the Internet in search of files that pertain to a topic of interest. A Gopher consists of menus of files, folders, and other Gophers. The fact that one Gopher knows about other Gophers on the Internet makes Gopher a good tool for searching the Internet. Often used to search for text files that can provide research information.

Gopherspace

A **Gopher** consists of menus of files, folders, and other Gophers. As a user moves about the Internet, traveling from Gopher to Gopher, the user is said to be traveling through Gopherspace.

home page

A Web **page** about a person or business. From someone's (or some place's) home page you can move about to other Web pages.

host

A computer on the Internet that you access. The host may hold files that you can **download** — often by **anonymous FTP**.

HTML (HyperText Markup Language)

The language that is used to design, or write, World Wide Web pages.

HTTP (HyperText Transfer Protocol)

The means by which a Web page is transferred across the Internet. When you use a **Web browser** to visit a Web, the contents of that page are transferred to your Macintosh using HTTP.

hypertext link

A World Wide Web **page** may include a word or picture or icon that, when clicked on, transfers the user to a completely different page.

Internet

The huge, worldwide network (or linkup) of government, business, and university computers.

mailing list

An e-mail address that is used as a *hub,* from which received e-mail messages are automatically re-sent to hundreds (sometimes thousands) of other people. A mailing list has a single topic, such as coin collecting or tropical fish care. Internet users subscribe to a mailing list and then correspond with one another by sending mail to the mailing list.

message

Newsgroups contain articles, or messages, posted, or sent, by individuals. Additionally, an **e-mail** note can be referred to as a message.

Navigator

The popular Web browsing software from **Netscape**.

Netscape

This is the company that developed the very popular Navigator Web browsing software.

newbie

A newcomer to the Internet.

newsgroup

An area of the Internet devoted to the exchange of information between Internet users who share a similar interest.

newsreader

A software program used to read and post messages found in a **newsgroup**. Commercial online services have newsreaders built into their access software.

NewsWatcher

Commercial online services come with access software that has built-in newsgroup-reading features. Local online services provide members with a combination of software programs for various tasks such as working with Internet newsgroups. NewsWatcher is one of the more popular newsgroup programs included in Internet software packages.

page

The World Wide Web is made up of millions of pages. Each page holds information concerning any topic imaginable. The information can appear in a variety of forms, including text, pictures, and icons. A World Wide Web page can include **hypertext links** — words or pictures that can be clicked on to transfer to a different page.

POP (Post Office Protocol)

A system used by a mail program on the Internet. POP allows a user to receive e-mail and download that mail to his or her own Macintosh.

PPP (Point-to-Point Protocol)

A system used to connect your Macintosh to the Internet using a phone line. PPP (or the similar **SLIP** system) is necessary if you're going to access the Internet directly — that is, without first going through the computer of a commercial online service such as **America Online** or **CompuServe**.

Prodigy

A commercial online service that is the result of a partnership between IBM and Sears. As a product of IBM, Prodigy's access software is understandably disconcerting to Mac enthusiasts.

.sit

The file extension for a file that has been compressed with the program StuffIt. Either StuffIt Expander or the program Compact Pro can be used to uncompress such a file.

SLIP (Serial Line Internet Protocol)

A system used to connect your Macintosh to the Internet using a phone line. SLIP (or the similar **PPP** system) is necessary if you're going to access the Internet without the use of a commercial online service such as **America Online** or **CompuServe**.

surfing the Net

Electronically traveling about the different areas of the Internet — especially the World Wide Web.

thread

A single message posted to a **newsgroup** is called an article. All of the articles that deal with a single topic comprise a thread.

TurboGopher

Commercial online services come with access software that has built-in Gopher searching features. Local online services provide members with a combination of software programs for various tasks such as performing Gopher searches. TurboGopher is one of the more popular Gopher programs included in Internet software packages.

URL (Uniform Resource Locator)

The format for naming an Internet resource, such as a Web page. While usually thought of as the address of a Web page, a URL can also describe the location of a **Gopher** server (site) or an **FTP** server (site).

Veronica

A **Gopher**-searching utility. Allows you to enter a keyword that is used in a search of **Gopherspace**.

WAIS (Wide Area Information Service)

Pronounced *ways,* this file-searching resource is used to look for files listed in large databases.

Web browser

A software program used to view World Wide Web pages. Also simply referred to as a browser.

Web page

See **page**.

World Wide Web

Or WWW, or the Web. A part of the Internet that allows for the display of graphics and text on pages, or screens, of information.

Index

IDG BOOKS WORLDWIDE REGISTRATION CARD

RETURN THIS REGISTRATION CARD FOR FREE CATALOG

Title of this book: The Internet For Macs™ For Dummies® QR, 2E

My overall rating of this book: ❏ Very good [1] ❏ Good [2] ❏ Satisfactory [3] ❏ Fair [4] ❏ Poor [5]

How I first heard about this book:

❏ Found in bookstore; name: [6]   ❏ Book review: [7]
❏ Advertisement: [8]   ❏ Catalog: [9]
❏ Word of mouth; heard about book from friend, co-worker, etc.: [10] ❏ Other: [11]

What I liked most about this book:

What I would change, add, delete, etc., in future editions of this book:

Other comments:

Number of computer books I purchase in a year: ❏ 1 [12] ❏ 2-5 [13] ❏ 6-10 [14] ❏ More than 10 [15]

I would characterize my computer skills as: ❏ Beginner [16] ❏ Intermediate [17] ❏ Advanced [18] ❏ Professional [19]

I use ❏ DOS [20] ❏ Windows [21] ❏ OS/2 [22] ❏ Unix [23] ❏ Macintosh [24] ❏ Other: [25]_____
(please specify)

I would be interested in new books on the following subjects:
(please check all that apply, and use the spaces provided to identify specific software)

❏ Word processing: [26]   ❏ Spreadsheets: [27]
❏ Data bases: [28]   ❏ Desktop publishing: [29]
❏ File Utilities: [30]   ❏ Money management: [31]
❏ Networking: [32]   ❏ Programming languages: [33]
❏ Other: [34]

I use a PC at (please check all that apply): ❏ home [35] ❏ work [36] ❏ school [37] ❏ other: [38] _____

The disks I prefer to use are ❏ 5.25 [39] ❏ 3.5 [40] ❏ other: [41]_____

I have a CD ROM: ❏ yes [42] ❏ no [43]

I plan to buy or upgrade computer hardware this year: ❏ yes [44] ❏ no [45]

I plan to buy or upgrade computer software this year: ❏ yes [46] ❏ no [47]

Name: _____ Business title: [48] _____
Type of Business: [49]
Address (❏ home [50] ❏ work [51]/Company name: _____)
Street/Suite#
City [52]/State [53]/Zipcode [54]: _____ Country [55] _____

❏ **I liked this book!**
You may quote me by name in future IDG Books Worldwide promotional materials.

My daytime phone number is _____

IDG BOOKS
THE WORLD OF COMPUTER KNOWLEDGE

❏ YES!

Please keep me informed about IDG's World of Computer Knowledge. Send me the latest IDG Books catalog.